ideas

ideas

+apartments
+apartamentos
+appartements
+wohnungen

AUTHORS
Fernando de Haro & Omar Fuentes

EDITORIAL DESIGN & PRODUCTION

EDITORES

PROJECT MANAGERS
Edali Nuñez Daniel
Laura Mijares Castellá

COORDINATION
Laura Mar Hernández Morales

PREPRESS COORDINATION
Carolina Medina Granados

COPYWRITER
Roxana Villalobos

ENGLISH TRANSLATION
Babel International Translators

FRENCH TRANSLATION
Architextos: Translation Services and Language Solutions

GERMAN TRANSLATION
Angloamericano de Cuernavaca
Sabine Klein

Ideas
+apartments . +apartamentos . +appartements . +wohnungen

© 2011, Fernando de Haro & Omar Fuentes

AM Editores S.A. de C.V.
Paseo de Tamarindos 400 B, suite 109, Col. Bosques de las Lomas,
C.P. 05120, México, D.F., Tel. 52(55) 5258 0279
E-mail: ame@ameditores.com   www.ameditores.com

ISBN: 978-607-437-086-7

Printed in China.

introduction   introducción

This book examines residential apartments and has been divided, in accordance with size and typology, into the following chapters: lofts, small apartments and spacious apartments.

Apart from this classification, the different topics are covered without following a specific order, the main aim being to unveil to readers the decisions taken by interior and other designers and decorators in order to achieve a given result in each space.

Esta publicación está dedicada al análisis de la vivienda en apartamentos. Los capítulos se han agrupado según su dimensión y tipología en: lofts, apartamentos chicos y apartamentos amplios.

Salvo dicha clasificación, los temas son abordados sin seguir un orden específico, y siempre tratando de evidenciar ante el lector las decisiones que han tomado los diseñadores, interioristas y decoradores para obtener determinados resultados en cada espacio.

introduction   einleitung

Cet ouvrage a pour thème les appartements en tant que logements. Leur taille et leur genre ont permis de les classer en trois catégories : lofts, petits appartements, grands appartements.

Si l'on excepte cette catégorisation, les thèmes de ce livre sont abordés sans ordre préétabli en essayant constamment de mettre en valeur les décisions des concepteurs de projet, des architectes d'intérieur et des décorateurs pour obtenir tel ou tel résultat dans chaque espace.

Dieses Buch widmet sich der Analyse des Lebens in einer Wohnung. Die einzelnen Kapitel sind, gemäss der Wohnungsgrösse und -art, gruppiert in: Loft Wohnungen, kleine Wohnungen und grosse Wohnungen.

Von dieser Unterteilung abgesehen folgen die behandelten Themen keiner speziellen Ordnung und bemühen sich stets dem Leser, die von den Designern, Innenarchitekten und Dekorateuren getroffenen Entscheidungen aufzuzeigen, die zu dem spezifischen Ergebnis in jedem einzelnen Wohnbereich geführt haben.

These pages also set out the main trends of the present day, namely the predominance of simplicity in the decor, as well as the current preference for creating balanced and harmonious settings based on pure lines, basic geometric shapes and color scales.

Readers can also see that, regardless of scale, the cutting edge of interior design now focuses on the creation of continuous, open and shared spaces that are easy to furnish, clean and arrange.

As far as architecture is concerned, current tastes favor free floors, double heights and large windows that let daylight flood in. As for artificial lighting, the emphasis is on leds in warm tones.

Overloaded decorations, patterns, over-elaborate designs and heavy volumes are on their way out, while lighter volumes, smooth wallpaper and the practical contributions of each item included in the decorative scheme are more in tune with the times.

A lo largo de las páginas se puede observar como principal característica de los tiempos actuales la sencillez en la decoración, así como la tendencia a conseguir ambientes en equilibrio y armonía a partir de líneas puras, formas geométricas básicas y gamas de colores.

De igual modo, es posible percatarse de que sin importar su escala, se ha puesto a la vanguardia la idea de generar espacios continuos, abiertos y compartidos, fáciles de amueblar, limpiar y organizar.

En lo que respecta a la arquitectura, se prefieren plantas libres, dobles alturas y extensos ventanales que permiten aprovechar la luz natural durante el día. En cuanto a la iluminación artificial, se percibe un mayor protagonismo del led en tonos cálidos.

Los excesos decorativos, los estampados, garigolas y los volúmenes pesados se perfilan a desparecer; por el contrario, la ligereza volumétrica, los tapices lisos y la

En feuilletant cet ouvrage, on peut constater que les tendances actuelles de la décoration se caractérisent par leur simplicité et par la recherche d'un certain équilibre, d'une certaine harmonie, avec des lignes pures, des formes géométriques basiques et des gammes déterminées de couleurs.

On peut également se rendre compte que les espaces ouverts, continus ou fractionnés, faciles à meubler, à entretenir et à organiser, ont le vent en poupe, et ce, quelle que soit leur taille initiale.

Quant à l'architecture du logement, la préférence va vers des grandes pièces avec double hauteur de plafond et de larges baies vitrées pour profiter de la lumière du jour. L'éclairage artificiel est, lui, assuré par des ampoules à led avec des tons chauds.

Autre tendance actuelle : une certaine légèreté volumétrique, des moquettes ou tapis lisses et une recherche de la fonctionnalité pour tous les éléments

Im Verlaufe des Buches ist zu bemerken, dass das aktuelle Hauptmerkmal in der Dekoration Schlichtheit ist, wie auch die Tendenz zu einem ausgewogenen und harmonischen Ambiente durch reine Linien, einfache geometrische Formen und dem gewähltem Farbspektrum.

Genauso kann man bemerken, dass ohne Berücksichtigung der Grösse, die Idee ineinander übergehende Bereiche zu schaffen, die offen sind und miteinander geteilt werden, leicht zu möblieren, sauber zu machen und zu organisieren sind, zur Avantgarde geworden ist.

Was die Architektur betrifft, werden freie Grundrisse bevorzugt, doppelte Höhe und ausgedehnte Fenster, die es erlauben das natürliche Licht während des Tages zu nutzen. Was die künstliche Beleuchtung betrifft, wird LED Leuchten in warmen Tönen die Hauptrolle zugestanden. Es zeichnet sich ab, dass übermässige Dekoration, Drucke und als schwer empfundene Volumen im

Bare materials in their natural state are also in vogue, the most commonly used being wood, stone, steel, glass and cement. There is also the new generation of plastic and acrylic laminations used to line plywood.

The finishes of surfaces in kitchens and bathrooms, tabletops, floors and walls now need to be very polished and matt, while textured rugs are the choice of professionals.

Many items of furniture are produced with modular designs that make them easy to transport and adapt to whichever activity they will be involved in at any given time. Examples of this include tables, stools, sofas and dining room tables that sometimes double up as desks.

It looks like the preference for simplicity is not a short-lived fad, but a style that has already been in vogue for fifteen years and is going to be around for several decades more.

The growing number of furniture and accessory producers has given rise to better options and lower prices for consumers, who now have a vast range of alternatives to choose from.

The aim of the texts and pictures in this book is to share this wealth of ideas and proposals with readers, along with some practical examples laying bare the secrets behind the results.

funcionalidad de cada elemento que se introduce en la escena decorativa se ha convertido en un signo de actualidad.

La exposición de los materiales en su estado natural es, asimismo, una inclinación del presente; siendo los más recurrentes la madera, la piedra, el acero, el vidrio y el cemento, además de la nueva generación de laminados de plástico y acrílico con los que se forran los aglomerados.

Los acabados de las cubiertas de cocinas y baños, mesas, pisos y muros se prefieren muy pulidos y mate, en tanto que los tapetes texturizados son preferidos por los profesionales.

Una buena parte de los muebles presentan diseños modulares que facilitan su traslado y son adaptados en función de la actividad que se realice en cada momento: es el caso de mesas auxiliares, taburetes, sofás, o incluso de mesas de comedor que a veces se convierten en escritorios.

Como se puede inferir, la preferencia por la simplicidad no parece ser una moda pasajera, sino un estilo que se impondrá por lo menos durante las siguientes décadas y que ya lleva en boga al menos quince años.

La cantidad de productores de muebles y accesorios ha dado lugar a mejores alternativas y precios para el consumidor, quien tiene para elegir entre un vasto abanico de posibilidades.

Ojalá que este cúmulo de ideas y propuestas que se van revelando entre textos e imágenes, desmenuzando y estudiando uno a uno los ejemplos prácticos, resulten en un aprendizaje para el lector.

jouant un rôle dans la décoration. En conséquence, les motifs imprimés trop lourds, les décorations impressionnantes et autres éléments massifs ont tendance à disparaître.

On n'hésite pas, non plus, maintenant, à exposer certains matériaux à l'état brut. Il s'agit le plus souvent du bois, de la pierre, de l'acier, du verre et du ciment mais aussi de la nouvelle génération de produits en plastique ou en acrylique que l'on utilise pour recouvrir l'aggloméré.

De même, pour ce qui relève des revêtements des cuisines, salles de bain, tables, sols et murs, on opte de nos jours pour des finitions mates et bien polies. Quant aux revêtements textiles des sols, les professionnels préfèrent ceux qui sont texturés.

Le mobilier est, lui, généralement modulaire pour le transporter et l'adapter facilement aux activités choisies. C'est le cas, par exemple, des tables d'appoint, des tabourets, des canapés, voire même des tables de la salle à manger qui peuvent parfois être utilisées comme bureaux.

On notera au passage que cette préférence vers la simplicité ne relève pas d'une mode passagère mais d'un véritable style qui restera présent dans les prochaines décennies, au moins, et qui existe déjà depuis une quinzaine d'années.

Qui plus est, le consommateur peut profiter de la large gamme de solutions proposées par un nombre importants de fabricants de meubles et d'accessoires tout en disposant d'un budget qui reste limité.

Avec cet ouvrage, nous espérons ainsi avoir atteint notre objectif : faire en sorte que le lecteur fasse son choix parmi cette très large gamme d'idées et de suggestions une fois qu'il aura vu toutes ces photos, lu tous ces textes et adopté ou rejeté les exemples proposés.

Verschwinden begriffen sind; im Gegensatz dazu haben sich Formen leichter Ausmasse, schlichte Textilien und die Funktionalität eines jeden Bestandteiles, das in den zu dekorierenden Bereich eingeführt wird, zu einem Merkmal für Aktualität entwickelt.

Die Verwendung von Materialien in ihrem natürlichen Zustand ist auch eine gegenwärtige Tendenz; Holz, Stein, Stahl, Glas und Beton, darüber hinaus die neue Generation von Plastik- und Acrylbeschichtungen mit denen das Gestein verkleidet wird, sind die am meisten verwendeten.

Die Verarbeitung der Oberflächen in Küchen und Badezimmern, Tischen, Böden und Wänden werden stark glänzend oder matt bevorzugt, so werden auch Teppiche mit Textur von professionellen Dekorateuren vorgezogen.

Ein grosser Teil der Möbel zeigt ein Design in unabhängigen Modulen, die das Umstellen erleichtern und sich an die jeweilige Aktivität anpassen lassen: das ist der Fall bei Beistelltischen, Hockern, Sofas oder sogar bei Esstischen, die sich in Schreibtische verwandeln lassen.

Wie man schliessen kann, ist die Bevorzugung der Schlichtheit nicht nur eine vorrübergehende Mode, sondern eine Stilrichtung, die sich mindestens in den nächsten Jahrzehnten zeigen wird und die bereits mindestens seit 15 Jahren präsent ist.

In der Produktion von Möbeln und Zubehör gibt es derzeit mehr Alternativen und bessere Preise für den Verbraucher, der zwischen einer weiten Bandbreite von Möglichkeiten wählen kann.

Bleibt zu wünschen, dass die Sammlung von Ideen und Vorschlägen, die in den Texten und Fotografien aufgezeigt werden, die praktischen Beispiele genau untersuchend und studierend, den Leser etwas lernen lässt.

lofts • loftwohnungen

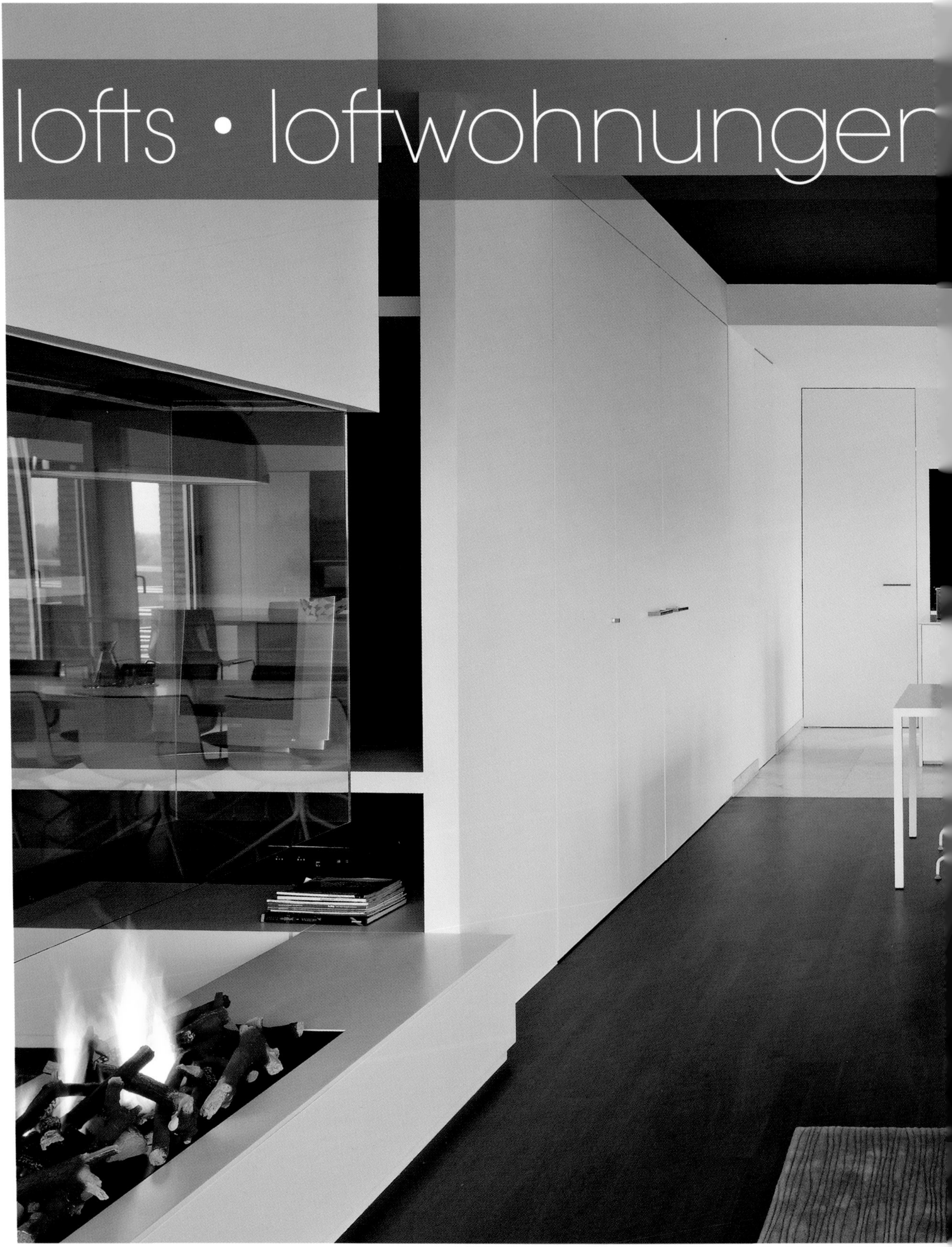

in motion
en movimiento
en mouvement
in bewegung

THE PUBLIC AND PRIVATE AREAS are floors without dividing walls or columns, which means all the different zones are arranged in a single continuum. The uniformity of such a setting can be guaranteed if the décor is confined to simple-lined furniture. The palette of colors in the living room is restricted to whites and browns, while in the bedroom yellow is used to do away with neutrality. The colors of the artwork stand out, while the sinuous shapes of certain decorative objects create an overall air of vitality.

LAS ÁREAS PÚBLICAS Y PRIVADAS son plantas sin muros intermedios ni columnas, lo que permite integrar todas las zonas en un continuo. Para homogeneizar el ambiente, la decoración se limita a muebles de líneas simples. En la estancia, la gama cromática se reduce a blancos y chocolate, en tanto que en la habitación se rompe la neutralidad con el amarillo. Sobresale el colorido del arte, y las formas sinuosas de algunos objetos decorativos le dan movimiento al conjunto.

AVEC DES PIÈCES COMMUNES OU PRIVÉES sans mur intermédiaire ni colonne, toutes les zones de l'espace sont intégrées en continu. Pour homogénéiser le tout, la décoration se limite à des lignes simples. Pour le salon, la gamme chromatique est circonscrite aux blancs et au chocolat alors que le jaune de la chambre a pour but de rompre cette neutralité. Quant au mouvement de l'ensemble, il est assuré par les couleurs plus vives de certains objets d'art ou des formes sinueuses de quelques objets décoratifs.

DIE ÖFFENTLICHEN UND PRIVATEN BEREICHE sind Etagen ohne Trennwände oder Säulen, was erlaubt alle Zonen fortlaufend ineinander zu integrieren. Um das Ambiente zu vereinheitlichen, ist die Dekoration auf Möbel mit einfachen Linien beschränkt. Im Wohnbereich reduziert sich das Farbspektrum auf Weiss- und Schokoladentöne, während im Schlafzimmer die Neutralität durch das Gelb gebrochen wird. Es sticht die Farbigkeit der Kunstwerke und die gewagten Formen einiger Dekorationsobjekte hervor, die dem Ganzen den Eindruck von Bewegung verleihen.

A GLASS DOOR JOINING THE SOCIAL AREA and the terrace merges the indoor and outdoor zones. A blend of styles affords vibrancy for the place, which is dominated by the smooth, soft surfaces of walls, ceilings and shelves. The inclusion of stainless steel and chrome, combined with the simple design, gives the setting an unmistakably modern look.

LA FUSIÓN INTERIOR-EXTERIOR se consigue con la puerta de vidrio que une la zona social con la terraza. La mezcla de estilos le imprime dinamismo al lugar. Los acabados lisos y suaves de muros, cubiertas y anaqueles dominan el área. La presencia del acero inoxidable y el cromo, sumados a la simplicidad en el diseño, le dan al ámbito una marcada apariencia actual.

LA FUSION INTÉRIEUR-EXTÉRIEUR est réussie grâce à la porte vitrée qui relie la pièce commune à la terrasse. Le mélange de styles divers dynamise les lieux. Les surfaces lisses et douces des murs, des revêtements et des étagères dominent l'espace. Et le fait que l'acier inoxydable et le chrome s'ajoutent à cette simplicité architecturale donne à la décoration un air très actuel.

DAS VERSCHMELZEN VON AUSSEN- UND INNENBEREICHEN wird mit der Glastür erreicht, die den gesellschaftlichen Bereich mit der Terrasse vereint. Die Mischung verschiedener Stilrichtungen prägt den Raum mit Dynamik. Die glatte und sanfte Verkleidung der Wände, Abdeckungen und Schränke dominiert die Zone. Die Präsenz von rostfreiem Stahl und Chrom, zusätzlich zu der Schlichtheit des Designs, geben dem Raum eine deutlich aktuelle Erscheinung.

decidedly today
decididamente actual
décidemment très actuel
entschlossen aktuell

The design of the furniture is simple and exquisitely finished. It also looks great thanks to the extraordinary ratio between its size and the extent of the double height space. The inside strives to echo the outside through carpets and rugs made with natural fibers and rugged textures, which provide warmth for the atmosphere. Green, the second most important color in the décor (after white), is present in the views of nature outdoors and in some of the decorative motifs used indoors.

El mobiliario presenta un diseño depurado y finos acabados; luce único gracias a la extraordinaria proporción que existe entre su dimensión y el amplio espacio a doble altura. El adentro intenta mimetizarse con el afuera, a través de alfombras y tapetes de fibras naturales y rugosas texturas que le brindan calidez a la atmósfera. Después del blanco, el verde es el color más significativo en el decorado, aparece tanto en las vistas que se tienen de la naturaleza exterior como en algunos motivos decorativos usados al interior.

De conception épurée avec ses surfaces traitées de manière très recherchée, le mobilier joue un rôle étonnant grâce à ses proportions en rapport avec l'espace très grand avec double hauteur de plafond. Les moquettes et les tapis de tissus rêches en fibres naturelles participent à l'effacement des frontières entre intérieur et extérieur et dotent la pièce d'une certaine qualité. Très présent dans la vue dehors et sur quelques motifs intérieurs, le vert est, après le blanc, la couleur la plus importante de cette décoration.

Die Möbel zeigen ein reines Design und feine Verarbeitung; sie treten nur duch das ausserordentliche Verhältnis zwischen ihren Ausmassen und dem weiten Raum in doppelter Höhe hervor. Der Innenraum versucht den Aussenbereich zu imitieren - durch die Auslegeware und Teppiche aus Naturfasern und rauer Textur, die dem Raum Wärme vermitteln. Nach Weiss ist Grün die bedeutendste Farbe in der Dekoration, sie findet sich sowohl in der Aussicht auf die Natur draussen, als auch in einigen dekorativen Motiven im Innenbereich.

art box • caja de arte • un véritable musée • kunstkasten

LARGE WINDOWS allow generous helpings of daylight to pour in and release the full visual potential of the place. The space is used to the full to create places for storage, including a huge bookshelf spanning the room's double height. The clean design brings out the decorative details, like a large box inhabited solely by art.

LOS GRANDES VENTANALES captan generosas entradas de luz natural y liberan las visuales. El espacio se aprovecha al máximo para generar sitios de guardado, incluyendo un librero monumental que abarca las dos alturas. La limpieza del diseño permite destacar los detalles decorativos, como si se tratara de una gran caja para que habite el arte.

LES GRANDES BAIES VITRÉES captent généreusement la lumière naturelle et libèrent la vue. L'espace est utilisé au maximum pour y placer des meubles de rangements, y compris avec une bibliothèque monumentale qui est aussi élevée que la double hauteur de plafond. Et ce design si propre et net permet de faire ressortir les détails décoratifs pour transformer cette pièce en véritable musée d'art.

DIE GROSSEN FENSTER lassen natürliches Licht grosszügig einfallen und setzen die optischen Reize frei. Der Bereich wird aufs äusserste Äusserste genutzt um Stauraum zu schaffen, einschliesslich eines riesigen Bücherregals, das sich über beide Etagen erstreckt. Die Reinheit des Designs erlaubt es einigen dekorativen Details herauszustechen, als ob es sich um einen grossen Kasten handeln würde, in dem die Kunst lebt.

vibrant and harmonious
rítmico y en paz
paisiblement rythmé
rhythmisch und ausgeglichen

The scheme used for wood affords it the lead role in the interior décor with its quality shining out in each space together with the meticulously executed details. The way different wooden items of similar breadths have been positioned to make headboards, closets, chests of drawers, the floor and furniture, bestows the space with a singular vibrancy. A few white walls aside, the palette of colors comprises different tones of the same material. The total absence of decorative objects affords the space a tangible sense of peacefulness.

El esquema usado para la madera la convierte en el elemento principal del interiorismo. En cada espacio se destaca la calidad del material y el cuidado en el detalle. La manera en la que han sido colocadas las piezas de madera de anchos similares para conformar cabeceras, clósets, cajoneras, piso y muebles, dotan de un ritmo único al espacio. Con excepción de algunos muros blancos, la paleta cromática está dada por la combinación tonal del mismo material. La total ausencia de objetos de ornato provoca que el espacio se sienta en paz.

Le rôle joué par le bois en fait l'élément le plus important de cette décoration. Chaque espace met en valeur la qualité du matériau et la finition des détails. La manière dont a été utilisé le bois au sol et pour fabriquer des chevets, des placards, des commodes, des meubles de largeur identique, donne un rythme unique à l'espace. Si l'on excepte quelques murs blancs, la palette chromatique associe les divers tons d'un même matériau. Et l'absence d'objets décoratifs confère à l'ensemble une atmosphère paisible.

Die Art in der das Holz verwendet wird macht es zum Hauptelement in der Dekoration. In jedem Bereich wird die Qualität des Materials und die Aufmerksamkeit, die den Details geschenkt wird, hervorgehoben. Die Art in der die einzelnen Holzdielen gleicher Breite angebracht sind, um Kopfstücke der Betten, Wandschränke, Kommoden, Boden und Möbel zu formen, geben dem Raum einen einzigartigen Rhythmus. Mit Ausnahme einiger weisser Wände, wird die Farbpalette von der Kombination des Materials selbst bestimmt. Die vollständige Abwesenheit jeglicher Dekorationsobjekte lassen den Raum ausgeglichen wirken.

PURE WHITE is serene and delicate. Its allure never ends. Giving it the prevalent position in the décor is a good move, because it enhances the visual sensation of spaciousness and floods the space with brightness. The whiteness of the bathroom and kitchen alike emphasizes order and cleanliness, and this sensation is taken to new heights by the inclusion of windows, mirrors and highly polished surfaces.

EL BLANCO PURO es sereno y delicado, es un color siempre vigente. Seleccionarlo como predominante de esta decoración es un acierto, pues logra aumentar la sensación visual de amplitud y brinda luminosidad espacial. La blancura del baño y la cocina subraya el efecto de limpieza y orden; esta evocación de pulcritud se acrecienta con la introducción de vidrios, espejos y cubiertas muy pulidas.

JAMAIS DÉMODÉ, LE BLANC PUR est une couleur sereine et délicate. L'avoir choisi pour dominer cette décoration constitue une belle réussite parce qu'il agrandit et illumine l'espace. Cette même couleur dans la cuisine et la salle de bain fait également ressortir l'aspect ordonné et propre de ces pièces. Et ce côté net est encore renforcé par les fenêtres, les miroirs et les revêtements très lisses.

REINES WEISS ist gelassen und delikat; es ist eine immer aktuelle Farbe. Als vorherrschende Farbe in dieser Einrichtung gewählt, ist sie ein voller Erfolg, da sie den optischen Eindruck von Weite vergrössert und räumliche Helligkeit bietet. Das Weiss des Badezimmers und der Küche unterstreicht den Eindruck von Sauberkeit und Ordnung; diese Beschwörung von Reinheit wird noch durch die Verwendung von Glas, Spiegeln und stark glänzenden Beschichtungen verstärkt.

pure white
blanco puro
blanc pur
reines weiss

WHITE, SIMPLE-LINED FURNITURE brings out the stylishness and simplicity of the kitchen-dining room area. Light-colored wood with a matt finish on the floor adds a welcome touch of warmth. In every area the furniture is distributed around the perimeter in order to make the most of the available space. Some items of furniture are used for storage. The kitchen's bars divide the living room but without undermining the continuity of this single space.

EL MOBILIARIO DE LÍNEAS SIMPLES EN BLANCO realza la elegancia y sobriedad de la cocina-comedor; la madera clara en acabado mate usada en el piso da el toque de calidez. En todas las áreas, los muebles son colocados perimetralmente con el fin de hacer rendir el área, algunos de ellos son aprovechados para guardado. Las barras de la cocina segmentan la estancia sin que se pierda la impresión de tratarse de un solo espacio.

LE MOBILIER BLANC À LIGNES SIMPLES fait ressortir l'élégance et la sobriété de la cuisine-salle à manger. Au sol, le bois clair et mat réchauffe l'ensemble. Dans tous les espaces, on a placé les meubles (certains d'entre eux pour y ranger des choses) contre les murs pour profiter de la superficie des pièces. Et les comptoirs de la cuisine divisent partiellement la pièce sans pour autant la fragmenter.

MÖBEL MIT SCHLICHTEN LINIEN IN WEISS heben die Eleganz und Nüchternheit der Küche mit Esszimmer hervor; das für den Boden verwendete helle Holz mit matter Oberfläche spendet einen Hauch Wärme. In allen Bereichen sind die Möbel an den Wänden angebracht um den Raum vollständig auszunutzen, einige werden als Stauraum verwendet. Die Tresen der Küche unterteilen den Bereich ohne den Eindruck eines einzigen Raumes zu zerstören.

visual geometry
geometría visual
géométrie visuelle
optische geometrie

THE LOFT HAS SCANT furniture and the items of furniture it does have blend in with the architectural design and its geometrical distribution. The visual focal points are concentrated in the large window and its views, as well as its monumental staircase which stands in the area like a sculpture thanks to its design and lightness. Mirrors enhance the sensation of depth, while the use of the same finish on the floor and walls creates an illusion of flow.

EL LOFT SE DISTINGUE por la intervención de pocos muebles, muy integrados al diseño arquitectónico y con una distribución geométrica. Los focos visuales se concentran en el gran ventanal y sus vistas, así como en la escalera monumental que, por su diseño y ligereza, se posa en el área como una obra escultórica. Los espejos cooperan a dar la impresión de mayor profundidad. El uso de un solo acabado en pisos y muros amplifica la ilusión de fluidez.

CE LOFT SE CARACTÉRISE par le nombre limité de ses meubles, aux formes géométriques, qui s'intègrent très bien dans l'ensemble de la décoration. La grande baie vitrée et la vue qu'elle offre retiennent notre attention tout comme l'escalier monumental qui, avec son design original et sa légèreté, prend l'apparence d'une sculpture. Les miroirs, quant à eux, approfondissent l'espace. Et le fait d'avoir eu recours à un seul type de finition pour les sols et les murs conforte la sensation de fluidité de l'ensemble.

DAS LOFT ZEICHNET SICH durch die Verwendung nur weniger Möbel aus, die sehr in das architektonische Design integriert und geometrisch angeordnet sind. Der optische Blickpunkt konzentriert sich auf das grosse Fenster und die Aussicht, sowie auf die monumentale Treppe, die, duch ihr Design und ihre Leichtigkeit, im Raum wie eine Skulptur posiert. Die Spiegel tragen zum Eindruck grösserer Tiefe bei. Das Verwenden von nur einer Verarbeitung bei Böden und Wänden vergrössert die Illusion von Flüssigkeit.

THE PLACE IS NOTEWORTHY because it displays the structural components of the architecture, harnessing industrial designs for domestic usage. The clean and stylish combination of black and gray is accentuated by the upholstery pattern on the dining room seating and the cushions in the living room. The furniture has been arranged in balanced series to create a finely poised cadence. The staircase is a visual focal point.

EL LUGAR SE CARACTERIZA por mostrar los elementos estructurales de la arquitectura, asimilando el diseño industrial al uso doméstico. La mezcla elegante y pulcra de blanco, gris y negro es acentuada por el dibujo de la tapicería de las sillas del comedor y los cojines de la sala. El acomodo de los muebles en series equilibradas genera una armónica cadencia. La escalera se convierte en un elemento focal.

L'ORIGINALITÉ DE CE LIEU RÉSIDE DANS le fait qu'elle ne dissimule pas les éléments de sa structure et qu'elle montre que l'on peut les utiliser dans la vie quotidienne. L'association élégante et distinguée du blanc, du gris et du noir est accentuée par l'étoffe des chaises de la salle à manger et par les coussins du salon. Un rythme harmonieux règne sur l'ensemble grâce aux meubles placés sous forme de séries équilibrées et les escaliers attirent notre regard.

DER ORT ZEICHNET SICH durch das Offenlegen der architektonischen Strukturen aus, Industriedesign an den Hausgebrauch anpassend. Die elegante und reine Mischung von Weiss, Grau und Schwarz wird durch die Muster der Esstischstühle und der Kissen im Wohnzimmer hervorgehoben. Die Anordnung der Möbel in ausgewogenen Gruppen erzeugt einen harmonischen Rhythmus. Die Treppe wird zum Blickfang.

structural look
estética estructural
esthétique structurelle
ästhetik der struktur

among sensual tones
entre sensuales matices
des teintes sensuelles
zwischen sinnlichen schattierungn

THE DECORATIVE SCHEME of this apartment is based exclusively on the color gray, including polished natural cement floors. This brings out the light brown tones of the sofa in the living room and the wood in the dining room. The atmosphere in the bedroom is awash with sensuality thanks to the earth tone fabric used to make the upholstery and bed covers. The design's honesty is evidenced by the decision to display the materials with their textures on view. A pair of Mies van der Rohe chairs give the room a great finishing touch.

EL ESCENARIO DECORATIVO de este departamento es totalmente agrisado, incluyendo los pisos de cemento natural pulido. Ello hace que en la estancia resalte el tono tabaco del sofá y el de la madera del comedor. En la recámara, los tejidos de las tapicerías y ropa de cama en matices térreos dotan de sensualidad a la atmósfera. La preferencia por exponer los materiales con sus texturas a la vista evoca franqueza en el diseño. Dos sillas Mies van der Rohe dan el toque a la sala.

ÉTANT DONNÉ que le gris domine totalement la décoration de cet appartement (y compris pour les sols en ciment naturel poli), la couleur tabac du canapé et du bois de la salle à manger n'en ressort que mieux. Dans la chambre, les teintes terre du tissu des rideaux et de la literie apportent de la sensualité aux lieux. Le fait de ne pas avoir cherché à dissimuler les matériaux et leurs textures particulières se traduit par une certaine sincérité dans la décoration. Deux chaises Mies van der Rohe singularisent, quant à elles, le salon.

DIE DEKORATIVE BÜHNE dieser Wohnung ist vollständig in Grau gehalten, einschliesslich des polierten Betonbodens. Dadurch sticht im Wohnbereich das Tabakbraun des Sofas und des Holzes im Esszimmer hervor. Im Schlafzimmer stiften die Möbelbezüge und die Bettwäsche in Erdtönen eine sinnliche Stimmung. Die Wahl, die Materialien mit Blick auf die ihnen eigene Textur auszustellen, erweckt den Eindruck von Ehrlichkeit im Design. Zwei Mies van der Rohe Stühle geben dem Wohnzimmer einen besonderen Reiz.

small apartments
apartamentos chicos
petits appartements
kleine wohnungen

a majestic air
con aire majestuoso
un air majestueux
mit würdevollem flair

A STYLISH AND REFINED AMBIENCE is generated thanks to a super combination of fragmented white on the floors, ceilings and walls, copper red on the upholstery and a few details in dark brown. Even though the area is small, the curtains lend it a majestic air. The furniture is staunchly uniform in style and distributed in sequence to create the impression that one zone simply merges into the other. The dining area boasts classical chrome wire seats.

UNA COMBINACIÓN EXCEPCIONAL de blanco roto en pisos, techos y muros, shedrón en los tapices y algunos detalles en café oscuro crean un contexto elegante y refinado. Aun cuando el área es pequeña, el cortinaje le da un aire de majestuosidad. Los muebles guardan uniformidad en el estilo y son distribuidos en secuencia dando la sensación de que una zona se prolonga en la otra. El comedor exhibe las clásicas sillas Wire cromadas.

CETTE ASSOCIATION EXCEPTIONNELLE entre le blanc cassé des sols, des plafonds et des murs, le brun-rouge des tentures et quelques détails marron foncé fait de l'ensemble un endroit élégant et raffiné. Même lorsque l'espace est restreint, les rideaux confèrent à la pièce un air majestueux. Les meubles, par leur style uniforme et leur disposition régulière, effacent les séparations entre les espaces. Et dans la salle à manger, on trouve les classiques chaises chromées Wire.

EINE AUSSERORDENTLICH KOMBINATION von gebrochenem Weiss auf Böden, Decken und Wänden, dem Rotbraun der Möbelbezüge und einigen Details in Dunkelbraun, schafft eine elegante und raffinierte Umgebung. Auch wenn der Raum klein ist, geben ihm die Vorhänge einen würdevollen Anstrich. Die Möbel bewahren Einheitlichkeit im Stil und sind in Intervallen angeordnet, wodurch der Eindruck erweckt wird, dass sich ein Bereich in den anderen ausdehnt. Im Esszimmer werden klassische Chrom Wire Stühle ausgestellt.

The headboard's design runs towards the closet as if it were a single uninterrupted component to create a super decorative effect.

El diseño de la cabecera se extiende hacia el clóset como si se tratara de un componente ininterrumpido, alcanzando un resultado decorativo soberbio.

La tête de lit, d'une forme telle qu'elle touche le placard, semble faire partie de cet élément et jouer le rôle majeur dans cette décoration superbe.

Das Design des Bettkopfstückes dehnt sich über den Wandschrank aus, als wenn es sich um ein ununterbrochenes Element handeln würde und damit ein hervorragendes dekoratives Resultat erzielend.

A CHAISE LONGUE is reminiscent of the classic past but, at the same time, very much in tune with the contemporary furniture. Light entering through the tall window is toned down by translucent material. The room's double height is emphasized by the curtains adorning some of the windows. The living room is discretely divided by a wooden lattice structure that leaves the visual flow intact. Movable lights bathe different points of the soffit in light.

UN CHAISE LONGUE recuerda el pasado clásico y concuerda con el resto del mobiliario de factura contemporánea. La luz que penetra por los ventanales está tamizada por telas translúcidas. Para resaltar la doble altura, algunas ventanas son adornadas con cortinas. La estancia es sutilmente dividida por una celosía de madera, que no interrumpe la sucesión visual. Unos platones con luminarias dirigibles se esparcen en diversos puntos del plafón.

SURVIVANCE D'UN CLASSICISME passé, la chaise longue s'intègre parfaitement dans un mobilier d'aspect contemporain. La lumière est tamisée par des fenêtres recouvertes de tissus translucides. Pour mettre en valeur la double hauteur de plafond, quelques rideaux sont placés sur des fenêtres. L'espace est subtilement divisé par une jalousie en bois qui ne nuit pas à la continuité visuelle. Quelques plafonniers supportant des lampes directionnelles complètent ici et là la décoration.

EINE CHAISE LONGUE erinnert an die klassische Vergangenheit und passt zu den restlichen Möbeln zeitgenössischer Herstellung. Das durch die Fenster einfallende Licht, wird durch die lichtdurchlässigen Stoffe gemildert. Um die doppelte Höhe zu betonen sind einige der Fenster mit Vorhängen versehen. Der Wohnbereich ist subtil mit einer Holzjalousie unterteilt, die die optische Fortsetzung nicht unterbricht. Einige Platten mit beweglichen Leuchten sind über verschiedene Punkte der Decke verteilt.

contemporary classic
clásico contemporáneo
classique contemporain
zeitgenössische klassik

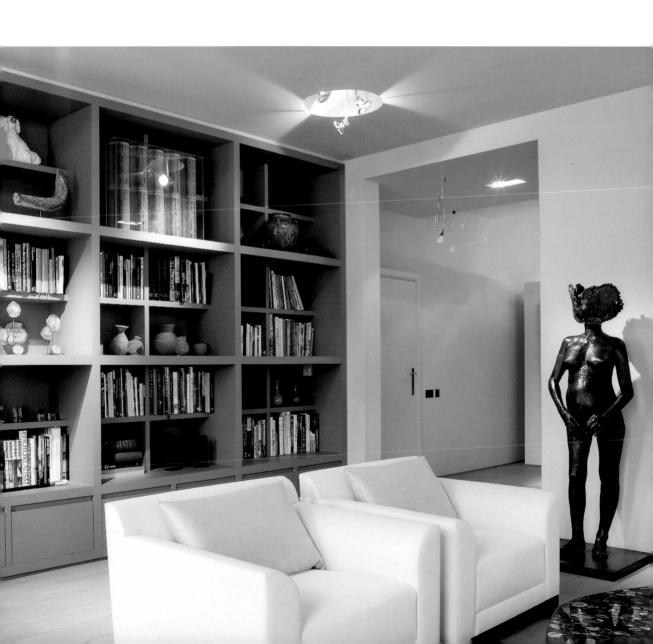

Two stools are the same color as the blue sofa and beige armchairs, acting as chromatic intermediaries and complementary living room furniture.

Dos taburetes comparten los colores del sofá azul y de los sillones beige, sirviendo como conectores cromáticos y como muebles complementarios de la sala.

Deux poufs reproduisent les couleurs bleu du canapé et beige des fauteuils afin d'assurer la continuation chromatique de l'espace et de compléter le mobilier du salon.

Die Hocker sind mit den gleichen Farben wie das blaue Sofa und die beigen Sessel bezogen und dienen damit als farbliche Verbindung und als ergänzende Wohnzimmermöbel.

comfortable and original
confortable y original
confortable et original
bequem und originell

The ambience is comfortable and pleasant in this small apartment thanks to the sumptuous furniture, the smooth upholstery and the prevalence of exquisitely veined wood on the floors and certain walls. The glass with lettering that marks one of bedroom's boundaries affords the décor a touch of originality and exhibits the occupant's favorite words.

El clima se percibe confortable y delicioso en este pequeño apartamento, gracias a los suntuosos muebles, a las suaves tapicerías y al dominio de una madera muy veteada en pisos y en determinados muros de remate. El cristal con tipografía que afora la habitación le da un toque original al decorado, y contiene textos predilectos.

Grâce à ses meubles somptueux, à ses tissus doux et au rôle majeur du bois particulièrement veiné pour les sols et pour certains murs importants, l'atmosphère délicieuse de ce petit appartement se caractérise par son confort. Le verre, avec la calligraphie particulière de ses textes incrustés, singularise le décor d'une pièce comme la chambre.

Das Raumklima wird in dieser kleinen Wohnung, dank der pompösen Möbel, der geschmeidigen Bezüge und der Vorherrschaft eines stark gemaserten Holzes auf Böden und an ausgesuchten Wänden als Abschluss, als bequem und charmant empfunden. Das mit ausgesuchten Texten beschriftete Kristall, das das Schlafzimmer unterteilt, gibt der Dekorationen einen Hauch Originalität.

daring and balanced
atrevido y equilibrado
audacieux mais équilibré
kühn und ausgewogen

STRIPED WALLPAPER is the most audacious feature of this room. The stripes' colors are repeated on the armchairs and the finishes of the dining room to create uniformity throughout. The lamp hanging above the middle of the dining room table and the glass item on the living room table account for most of the area's vitality. The textured rug and the fireplace are significant focal points.

EL TAPIZ A RAYAS SOBRE MURO es el elemento más atrevido de la estancia. Los colores de las rayas se repiten en los sillones y en los acabados del comedor generando una composición unitaria. Las piezas que mayor movimiento le otorgan al área son la lámpara que cuelga al centro de la mesa del comedor y el objeto de vidrio que yace sobre la mesa de la sala. El texturizado del tapete y la chimenea se constituyen también en puntos focales.

LES MOTIFS À RAYURES DU MUR constituent l'élément le plus audacieux de l'appartement. Les couleurs de ces rayures sont répétées sur les fauteuils et sur la surface de certains éléments pour harmoniser l'ensemble. Les éléments qui donnent le plus de mouvement à l'espace sont la lampe suspendue au-dessus du centre de la table et l'objet en verre sur la table basse. La texture du tapis et de la cheminée attirent également l'œil de l'observateur.

DIE GESTREIFTE TAPETE ist das kühnste Element im Wohnbereich. Die Farben der Streifen wiederholen sich in den Sesseln und in der Essgruppe, somit eine einheitlich Komposition schaffend. Die Stücke, die dem Bereich am meisten Bewegung verleihen, sind die über dem Tisch hängende Lampe und das Glasobjekt, das auf dem Wohnzimmertisch ruht. Die Textur des Teppichs und der Kamin erregen auch die Aufmerksamkeit.

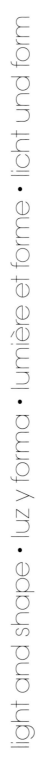

light and shape • luz y forma • lumière et forme • licht und form

A PROMINENT ASPECT of this apartment's design is the affinity between the geometric shapes of the ceiling and floor. The soffits have been built with different heights and contain light sources that give the area its charm. The furniture comes in tones akin to red wine to provide warmth, together with the wooden floor. A remarkable sculpture in the middle of the space and two eye-catching armchairs in floral upholstery emphasize the division of this space and are the jewels in the room's crown.

SE SUBRAYA EN EL DISEÑO de este apartamento la afinidad entre las formas geométricas del techo y del suelo. Los plafones están construidos a diversas alturas y contienen fuentes de luz, que le brinda un encanto al área. La calidez proviene del mobiliario en sobrios matices tintos y la duela del piso. Una escultura con gran movimiento localizada al centro del espacio y dos protagónicos sillones que coronan la sala, tapizados en estampado floral, refuerzan la división espacial.

LES FORMES GÉOMÉTRIQUES du plafond qui s'associent à merveille avec celles du sol caractérisent le design de cet appartement. Les plafonds sont de hauteurs diverses et les sources de lumière qui y sont encastrées esthétisent l'endroit. Le mobilier, avec ses couleurs vin et les motifs au sol, réchauffe les lieux. Une sculpture aux formes dynamiques au centre de l'espace ainsi que deux fauteuils avec un tissu à fleurs couronnant le salon soulignent la disposition fractionnée de l'endroit.

IN DIESER WOHNUNG wird die Stimmigkeit zwischen den geometrischen Formen der Decke und dem Boden unterstrichen. Die Platten sind in unterschiedlicher Höhe angebracht und enthalten Lichtquellen, die dem Raum Charme verleihen. Wärme kommt von den Möbeln in nüchternen Rottönen und den Bodendielen. Eine Skulptur mit viel Bewegung im Zentrum des Raumes und zwei die Aufmerksamkeit erregende Sessel, mit Bezügen in Blumenmuster, die das Wohnzimmer veredeln, verstärken die optische Unterteilung.

serenity with light
serenidad con luz
la sérénité de la lumière
gelassenheit mit licht

THE SENSATION OF SPACIOUSNESS and peacefulness is accentuated by the exclusive use of cream and brown tones. The quality of daylight is ideal for using dark tones on floors and walls. Given that it is a small space, a central track makes sure that light in the living - dining room is as uniform as possible. A small number of objects, in proportion with the whole, are on display as the finishing touches to the décor.

SE CONSIGUE AUMENTAR LA SENSACIÓN de amplitud y serenidad al restringir los matices a cremas y cafés. La calidad de la iluminación natural permite el uso de tonos oscuros en los recubrimientos de muros y pisos. Al tratarse de un espacio pequeño, un riel central asegura que la iluminación de la sala-comedor sea homogénea. Pocos objetos, que mantienen proporción con el conjunto, se despliegan completando la decoración.

EN SE LIMITANT AUX TEINTES crème et marron, l'espace s'en trouve agrandi et on met en valeur la sérénité de la pièce. Un éclairage naturel de qualité permet également l'utilisation de couleurs foncées pour le revêtement des murs et des sols. Lorsque l'appartement est petit, des lampes sur rail au centre éclairent tout le salon-salle à manger de manière homogène. Et quelques objets seulement donnent une certaine proportion à l'ensemble et complètent la décoration.

MAN KANN DURCH DIE BESCHRÄNKUNG auf Creme- und Kaffeetöne eine Verstärkung des Eindrucks von Weite und Gelassenheit erreichen. Die Qualität der natürlichen Beleuchtung erlaubt die Nutzung von dunklen Tönen in der Verkleidung von Wänden und Böden. Da es sich um einen kleinen Bereich handelt, sichert eine zentrale Schiene die gleichmässige Beleuchtung des Wohn- Esszimmers. Wenige Objekte, die in Proportion zum Ganzen stehen, vervollständigen die Dekoration.

balanced space
equidad espacial
équilibre spatial
räumliche ausgewogenheit

A SENSATION OF SPACIOUSNESS can be achieved by arranging all the different areas in a single overall space with the same style, color, finishes and materials. The only way to distinguish one area from another is by the function performed by the furniture. The décor has been designed by an even hand with no particular visual component standing out from the rest. The size of the lamp hanging above the dining table is an effective counterweight to the presence of the shelves on the far side of the room.

PARA DAR EL EFECTO DE MAYOR ESPACIALIDAD todas las zonas se integran en un solo conjunto compartiendo estilo, colorido, acabados y materiales; solamente se distingue una de otra por la funcionalidad del mobiliario. El decorado es parejo, sin sobresaltos visuales, sin protagonismos. La dimensión de la lámpara que descuelga sobre el comedor nivela el peso visual que ejerce el librero ubicado al lado opuesto.

AFIN DE DONNER PLUS D'ESPACE à toutes les zones d'un appartement, il est préférable d'opter pour un style, une couleur, un type de surface et des matériaux identiques partout. La fonctionnalité du mobilier sera le seul élément qui singularisera chacune des pièces. La décoration est donc uniforme, sans fracture visuelle et sans élément jouant un trop grand rôle. La lampe de grande taille dans la salle à manger sert, elle, à compenser le poids visuel pris par la bibliothèque dans le fond.

UM EINEN GRÖSSEREN RÄUMLICHEN Eindruck zu erreichen, bilden alle Bereiche ein Ensemble, in dem sie Stil, Farbe, Verarbeitung und Material teilen; nur ihre Funktion unterscheidet sie voneinander. Die Dekoration ist ebenmässig, ohne optische Überraschungen, ohne Blickfänge. Die Grösse der Lampe über dem Esstisch gleicht das optische Gewicht des Bücherregals ihr gegenüber aus.

THIS SMALL APARTMENT takes full advantage of the direct view of the sea through sliding doors with blinds that are also wonderful for regulating ventilation and sunlight. White is omnipresent, dominating walls, floors and ceilings. The cushions play a vital role in making the room look comfortable, while the straight-lined furniture sports white cotton upholstery. The room is also graced by two Mies van der Rohe armchairs.

ESTE PEQUEÑO APARTAMENTO aprovecha la vista directa al mar a través de puertas corredizas de persiana, que también cooperan a la ventilación y al control de la incidencia solar. El blanco abraza totalmente al espacio; está presente en muros, pisos y techos. La cojinería es determinante para que el lugar vivifique la impresión de comodidad. Los muebles de líneas rectas están tapizados en algodón blanco. Dos bancos Mies van der Rohe armonizan en la habitación.

AVEC CE PETIT APPARTEMENT, on profite de la vue directe sur la mer grâce aux portes coulissantes et à leurs stores. Ces derniers servent également à aérer et à limiter les rayons du soleil. Le blanc, présent sur les murs, au sol et au plafond, illumine littéralement l'espace. Les coussins jouent un rôle majeur pour donner à la pièce une sensation de confort. Les meubles, à lignes droites, sont tapissés de coton blanc et deux tabourets Mies van der Rohe harmonisent la chambre.

DIESE KLEINE WOHNUNG nutzt den direkten Blick aufs Meer durch seine Jalousieschiebetüren, die ausserdem zu einer besseren Belüftung beitragen und den Sonneneinfall kontrollieren. Das Weiss umarmt den Raum vollständig; es ist an Wänden, Böden und Decken präsent. Die Kissen sind entscheidend dafür, dass der Ort einen lebendigen und behaglichen Eindruck macht. Die Möbel mit geraden Linien sind mit weisser Baumwolle bezogen. Zwei Mies van der Rohe Hocker harmonisieren im Raum.

visual strategy
estrategia visual
stratégie visuelle
optische strategie

THE CHOICE OF LARGE SURFACES with light and dark tones in equal proportions was the key to achieving spatial harmony. A couple of details in bright red strategically placed in different points in the room guide the eye from one side to the other and force the viewer to examine the whole room. The furniture is mounted and fixed to the wall. The aim of using pale tones for the kitchen furniture is to underscore its independence from the living - dining room.

PARA CONSEGUIR ARMONÍA ESPACIAL se opta porque las grandes superficies cuenten con la misma proporción de tonos oscuros que de claros. Algunos elementos en rojo intenso, que son distribuidos estratégicamente en distintos puntos, llevan la vista de un lado al otro y obligan a realizar un recorrido del espacio. Los muebles se adosan y empotran a muros. Con la idea de subrayar la independencia de la sala-comedor, los gabinetes de la cocina son de madera clara.

POUR QU'UNE CERTAINE HARMONIE règne, il faut équilibrer les teintes claires et foncées pour les grandes surfaces. Quelques éléments en rouge vif sont stratégiquement distribués afin d'attirer notre attention et nous obliger à parcourir des yeux l'ensemble de la pièce. Les meubles, eux, sont encastrés dans le mur ou reposent sur ce dernier. Et pour vraiment faire du salon-salle à manger une pièce à part, les placards de la cuisine sont peints en marron clair.

UM RÄUMLICHE HARMONIE ZU ERREICHEN wählt man dunkle und helle Tönen in gleicher Proportion für grosse Flächen. Einige Elemente in intensivem Rot, strategisch über bestimmte Punkte verteilt, leiten den Blick von einem Punkt zum Anderen und zwingen zu einer optischen Reise durch den Raum. Die Möbel sind an die Wände angelehnt oder in ihnen eingebettet. Mit der Absicht die Unabhängigkeit des Wohn- Esszimmers zu unterstreichen, sind die Schränke der Küche aus hellem Holz.

SPACE IS FREED UP in the kitchen, living room and dining room by fixing furniture to the wall and leaving the central areas for tables. Three neutral scales –black, white and gray– are used to pacify the explosive blood red present in the sophisticated brocades of the upholstery, kitchen furniture, cushions and other adornments. This is without doubt a very courageous move for a small apartment, but it works well by balancing the visual impact of the different volumes.

PARA GANAR ESPACIO, igual en la cocina que en la sala y el comedor, los muebles se colocan adosados a muros, dejando las mesas al centro. Tres gamas neutras –negro, blanco y gris– se usan para serenar la energía del rojo sangre, que aparece en los sofisticados brocados de las tapicerías, en los muebles de cocina, cojines y otros objetos de ornato. Sin duda, la solución es audaz para un departamento pequeño, pero queda bien resuelta al balancear los pesos volumétricos.

POUR GAGNER DE LA PLACE aussi bien dans la cuisine que dans la salle à manger, les meubles sont disposés contre les murs avec les tables au milieu. Les trois couleurs neutres sélectionnées (noir, blanc et gris) atténuent le dynamisme du rouge sang des brocarts, des meubles de la cuisine, des coussins et de quelques autres objets décoratifs. Il ne fait aucun doute que la décoration choisie pour ce petit appartement est audacieuse mais elle est réussie grâce à un bon équilibre des poids volumétriques.

UM RAUM ZU GEWINNEN, in der Küche sowie im Wohnzimmer und im Esszimmer, sind die Möbel in die Wände eingebettet, die Tische im Zentrum lassend. Drei neutrale Farbpaletten – Schwarz, Weiss und Grau – werden benutzt um die Energie des Blutrots zu beruhigen, das in dem raffinierten Brokat der Bezüge, der Küchenmöbel, Kissen und anderen Zierobjekten erscheint. Ohne Zweifel ist diese Lösung für eine kleine Wohnung verwegen, aber sie funktioniert durch die Ausgewogenheit der einzelnen Volumen.

audacious and sophisticated
audaz y sofisticado
audacieux et recherché
verwegen und raffiniert

ONE GOOD DESIGN OPTION for an apartment by the sea involves using furniture made with natural fibers that announce their allegiance to local nature. This can be done with headboards, the backrests of seating and other ornate objects in this apartment. The décor is provided by artwork featuring marine landscapes, shells and cushions in sea tones.

UNA OPCIÓN DE DISEÑO para un departamento frente al mar es incluir mobiliario de fibras naturales, que recuerden su similitud con la naturaleza del lugar; es el caso de cabeceras, respaldos de sillas y algunos objetos de ornato de este departamento. El detalle decorativo se da a partir de cuadros de paisajes marinos, conchas y cojines con los tonos del mar.

POUR UN APPARTEMENT QUI DONNE sur la mer, on préférera un mobilier fabriqué en fibres naturelles pour qu'il s'intègre bien dans le paysage environnant. Ce matériau a été choisi dans cet appartement pour la tête de lit, les dossiers des chaises et quelques objets ornementaux. Quant aux coussins et aux tableaux reproduisant des coquillages ou des motifs marins, leurs couleurs soulignent la proximité des lieux avec la mer.

EINE MÖGLICHKEIT für eine Wohnung am Meer ist es, Möbel aus Naturfasern mit einzubeziehen, die ihre Ähnlichkeit mit der Natur des Ortes in Erinnerung bringen; in dieser Wohnung sind es die Kopfstücke der Betten, Stuhllehnen und einige Zierobjekte. Dekorative Details werden durch Gemälde mit Meermotiven, Muscheln und Kissen in Meerfarbtönen geliefert.

by the sea
frente al mar
face à la mer
am meer

light and shade
claroscuro
clair-obscur
hell und dunkel

LARGE WINDOWS through which plenty of light pours in are the reason why dark tones can be used for the furniture and walls and define the interior design in terms of the interplay between light and shade. The stylish combinations chosen include gray, black and brick red for the public area; and gray, red and steel blue for the private area. The floor comprises large wooden boards and the only objects occupying this space are works of art.

LOS MATICES OSCUROS en mobiliario y muros son factibles gracias a los ventanales, que permiten generosas entradas de luz, convirtiendo la escena de interiorismo en un claroscuro. Las combinaciones seleccionadas son muy elegantes, gris, negro y ladrillo para la zona pública; y gris, rojo quemado y azul acero para la privada. El suelo se conforma de grandes tablones de madera y los únicos objetos que habitan el espacio son piezas de arte.

LES MURS ET LE MOBILIER ont une teinte sombre grâce aux stores qui laissent passer une grande quantité de lumière mais qui permettent néanmoins cette décoration claire-obscure. L'élégance des associations de couleurs (gris, noir et brique pour les pièces communes, gris, rouge foncé et bleu métallisé pour les pièces privées) est indéniable. Le parquet est composé de grandes lattes de bois et les seuls objets dans l'appartement sont des œuvres d'art.

DIE DUNKLEN SCHATTIERUNGEN der Möbel und Wände sind dank der grossen Fenster möglich, die einen freizügigen Lichteinfall erlauben, damit den Schauplatz der Innendekoration in ein Spiel zwischen hell und dunkel verwandelnd. Die gewählten Kombinationen sind sehr elegant, Grau, Schwarz und Ziegelrot für die öffentlichen Bereiche; und Grau, gebranntes Rot und Stahlblau für die Privaten. Der Boden besteht aus grossen Holzdielen und die einzigen in den Räumen zu findenden Objekte sind Kunstwerke.

lively and practical • vivaz y práctico
plein de vie et pratique • lebendig und praktisch

VERMILION LIVENS UP a very even range of beiges that prevail in this space. The décor is simple and free of any excesses. Arranging the seating in an "L" shape makes the most of the available area, while a bench built into the wall completes the dining room seating. A vase, a couple of small tables in the living room and the dining room's seats reveal the degree of care that has gone into the details. The atmosphere is eased up by the views of the sea.

EL BERMELLÓN LE DA VIVACIDAD a una gama muy pareja de beiges que inunda el espacio. La decoración es limpia, sin objetos superfluos. El área se aprovecha con la disposición de los sillones en "L", y una banca empotrada que completa la sillería del comedor. El florero, el par de mesitas de apoyo en la sala y las sillas del comedor, denotan que hay cuidado en el detalle. Las vistas francas hacia el mar le confieren soltura al ambiente.

LE VERMILLON DONNE DE LA VIVACITÉ à la gamme très limitée des beiges qui dominent l'espace. La décoration est nette, sans objet superflu. On profite bien de l'endroit grâce aux coussins qui sont placés en « L » et une banquette encastrée complète les sièges de la salle à manger. Le vase, les deux petites tables dans le salon et les chaises de la salle à manger montrent que l'on fait attention aux détails. Et la vue dégagée sur la mer agrandit les pièces.

DAS ZINNOBERROT SPENDET dem Spektrum von sehr ähnlichen Beigetönen, das den Raum überflutet, Leben. Die Dekoration ist rein, ohne überflüssige Objekte. Der Raum wird durch die Position der Sessel in "L" Form und einer in der Wand eingebetteten Bank, die die Bestuhlung des Esszimmers vervollständigt, genutzt. Die Blumenvase, das Paar Beistelltische im Wohnzimmer und die Stühle des Esszimmers zeigen, dass den Details Aufmerksamkeit geschenkt wurde. Der offene Blick aufs Meer verleiht dem Raum Zwanglosigkeit.

longitudinal splendor
soberbia longitudinal
tout en longueur
lange pracht

ONE EFFECTIVE WAY to deal with a narrow space with depth in certain places is to fix storage furniture along the full length of the wall passing through the kitchen, dining room and living room, becoming part of the architecture and including other functional components such as a fireplace. The concealed light that emerges from behind this piece of furniture affords the area a particular charm. The spilt level marks the boundary between the living room and the dining room. The finishing touch in the living room is a classic Le Corbusier chaise longue.

COMO SOLUCIÓN para responder a una superficie angosta y profunda en pequeños espacios, se adosa a todo lo largo del muro un mueble de guardado que atraviesa cocina, comedor y sala, integrándose a la arquitectura e incorporando otros elementos funcionales, como es el caso de la chimenea. La iluminación oculta que emana de este mueble le confiere un particular atractivo al área. Un desnivel sirve para marcar el paso de sala a comedor; el remate de la sala es un clásico chaise longue Le Corbusier.

LORSQU'ON DISPOSE d'un petit appartement étroit mais profond, on aura soin de placer le meuble de rangement contre le mur traversant la cuisine, la salle à manger et le salon pour respecter l'architecture des lieux. On peut aussi ajouter quelques éléments fonctionnels comme une cheminée. L'éclairage dissimulé dans cette dernière met bien en valeur la pièce. Les marches servent à diviser la salle à manger et le salon avec sa chaise longue classique signée Le Corbusier.

ALS LÖSUNG FÜR einen engen und langgezogenen Grundriss mit kleiner Oberfläche baut man über die gesamte Länge der Wand einen Schrank, der sich über Küche, Esszimmer und Wohnzimmer erstreckt, in die Architektur integriert ist und andere funktionelle Elemente einbezieht, wie es bei dem Kamin der Fall ist. Die verdeckte Beleuchtung aus diesem Möbel gibt dem Bereich besondere Attraktivität. Ein Höhenunterschied markiert den Übergang zwischen Wohn- und Esszimmer; der Abschluss im Wohnzimmer ist eine klassische Le Corbusier Chaise Longue.

ONE DECORATIVE OPTION for making the most of the space involves using two chaise longues instead of living room furniture. Upholstery that is soft to the touch, some good fluffy cushions and a floor lamp turn the area into somewhere you'll enjoy reading in. The furniture in this room is complemented by a small table. The range of colors is limited and shared throughout the living room.

UNA POSIBILIDAD DECORATIVA que permite aprovechar el espacio es colocar dos chaise longues para sustituir la sala. Las tapicerías suaves al tacto, unos buenos cojines mullidos y la lámpara de pie provocan que el área se antoje como un lugar favorito para la lectura. Una pequeña mesa de trabajo se integra al amueblado de la zona. La paleta cromática es limitada y compartida en toda la estancia.

LORSQUE L'ESPACE EST RESTREINT, on peut placer deux canapés chaises longues pour créer un coin salon. Une housse douce au toucher, des coussins moelleux de bonne qualité et une lampe à pied transforment le lieu pour en faire un endroit propice à la lecture. La petite table de travail s'intègre au reste du mobilier. Quant à la palette chromatique, elle reste limitée et c'est la même dans tout l'appartement.

EINE MÖGLICHKEIT IN DER EINRICHTUNG, die die volle Nutzung des Raumes ermöglicht, ist es zwei Chaise Longue zu verwenden, die die Wohnzimmergarnitur ersetzen. Die weichen Bezüge, einige gute, weiche Kissen und die Stehlampe lassen den Bereich als perfekten Platz zum Lesen erscheinen. Ein kleiner Arbeitstisch integriert sich in die Einrichtung des Raumes. Die Farbpalette ist eingeschränkt und gleichmässig über den gesamten Wohnbereich.

decorative and practical
decorativo y práctico
décoratif et pratique
dekorativ und praktisch

A large painting covering most of the main wall floods the kitchen with color. The isle prompts the area to harbor aspirations as a hall and also provides somewhere for eating meals.

Un cuadro de gran formato, que casi cubre el muro principal, le da colorido a la cocina. La isla sirve para vestibular el área y al mismo tiempo cumple con la función de antecomedor.

Un tableau de grand format recouvrant presque tout le mur principal apporte de la couleur dans la cuisine. L'îlot central organise la pièce et sert à séparer la cuisine de la salle à manger.

Ein grosses Gemälde, das fast die gesamte Hauptwand bedeckt, gibt der Küche Farbe. Die Kücheninsel bringt den Bereich ins Gleichgewicht und erfüllt gleichzeitig die Funktion eines Anrichtetisches.

neutral tranquility
neutra quietud
une sérénité neutre
neutrale ruhe

THE SETTING IS NEUTRALIZED BY A BLEND of straw and light brown tones that invoke tranquility. The floor comprises wide, pale, wooden boards, displaying their discrete veining. The foot stools and armchair in the private areas convey the comfort of classic furniture. The bathroom furniture is dominated by right angles.

UNA MEZCLA DE TONOS PAJIZO Y AVELLANA neutraliza el contexto y evoca quietud. El piso son tablones de madera clara de anchos generosos, lo que provoca el lucimiento del discreto veteado. La piecera y el sillón de lectura de las áreas privadas recuerdan el confort de los muebles clásicos. El mobiliario de baño es predominantemente de ángulos rectos.

L'ASSOCIATION DE TEINTES NEUTRES (paille et noisette) dote l'endroit de sérénité. Le parquet est fait à partir de larges lattes de bois clair, ce qui met en valeur les discrètes veines naturelles. Le pouf repose-pieds et le fauteuil de lecture dans la pièce privée rappellent les meubles classiques confortables. Dans la salle de bain, le mobilier est principalement à angles droits.

EINE MISCHUNG AUS STROH- UND HASELNUSSTÖNEN neutralisiert die Umgebung und erweckt Ruhe. Der Boden besteht aus hellen, grosszügig breiten Holzdielen, die die unaufdringliche Maserung hervorheben. Die Bank am Bettende und der Lesesessel in den privaten Bereichen erinnern an den Konfort klassischer Möbel. Die Badezimmermöbel sind hauptsächlich rechtwinkelig.

spacious apartments
apartamentos amplios
grands appartements
grosse wohnungen

warm modernity · cálida modernidad
une chaude modernité · warme moderne

FOUR BROWN LEATHER CHAIRS team up alongside two white sofas to furnish the living room, which is reminiscent of the splendor of design in the 1950s. The hanging chandeliers, also from that period, provide the dining room with a singular charm. The living room features a wall that contradicts the prevalent tones for decorative purposes, as well as defining access to this part of the house. A noteworthy detail in the bedroom is the bed's base, which is part of the same component as the headboard.

CUATRO SILLAS DE PIEL CAFÉ acompañan a dos sofás blancos para conformar una sala, que recuerda el esplendor del diseño de los cincuenta. Los candiles colgantes, también de época, le dan un particular encanto al comedor. Para dividir el acceso de la estancia se integra a la arquitectura un muro que rompe con los tonos dominantes y tiene funciones decorativas. En la habitación destaca la base de la cama, que forma una sola pieza con la cabecera.

QUATRE SIÈGES EN CUIR MARRON et deux canapés blancs constituent la décoration du salon dont la splendeur rappelle celle des années 50. Les lustres, également d'époque, apportent un charme particulier à la salle à manger. Pour diviser l'appartement, une cloison est utilisée. Jouant un rôle décoratif, sa couleur rompt avec celles qui dominent dans les pièces attenantes. Dans la chambre, on remarquera la base et la tête de lit qui ne forment qu'un tout.

VIER BRAUNE LEDERSTÜHLE BEGLEITEN zwei weisse Sofas um eine Sitzgruppe zu bilden, die an den Glanz des Designs der fünfziger Jahre erinnert. Die Kronleuchter, aus der gleichen Epoche, geben der Essgruppe einen speziellen Charme. Um den Zugang zum Wohnbereich zu unterteilen ist eine Mauer in die Architektur integriert, die mit den dominierenden Farbtönen bricht und eine dekorative Funktion erfüllt. Im Schlafzimmer sticht der Bettrahmen hervor, der mit dem Kopfstück ein einziges Möbel bildet.

open to the sea
abierta al mar
une ouverture sur la mer
offen zum meer

THE AIM OF THE DESIGN is to merge indoors and outdoors. The living room is therefore fully merged with the terrace and open to the sea to achieve a rare spatial quality. The seat rests are made with natural fibers and combine superbly with the cotton in the upholstery and bed clothes. The living room's mahogany ceiling highlights the presence of the stone floor.

LA PREMISA DE DISEÑO parte de la intención de conectar el interior con el exterior. Así, la estancia queda totalmente unida a la terraza y abierta al mar, y se consigue una calidad espacial que no es habitual. Los textiles de los respaldos de las sillas son de fibras naturales, combinan estupendo con los algodones de las tapicerías y la ropa de cama. El techo caoba de la estancia resalta del piso pétreo.

L'IDÉE À LA BASE DE LA DÉCORATION consiste à relier l'extérieur avec l'intérieur. L'appartement est donc entièrement ouvert sur la terrasse et la mer avec pour résultat un espace de qualité que nous ne sommes pas habitués à voir. Les dossiers des sièges sont recouverts de fibres naturelles et ils s'associent merveilleusement avec le coton des canapés et du lit. Et le plafond en acajou du séjour met en valeur le marbre du sol.

DIE VORGABE IM DESIGN ist der Versuch den Innenbereich mit dem Aussenbereich zu verbinden. So ist der Wohnbereich komplett mit der Terrasse verbunden und zum Meer hin offen wodurch eine ungewöhnliche räumliche Qualität erreicht wird. Die Stoffe der Stuhlrücken sind aus Naturfasern, sie kombinieren hervorragend mit der Baumwolle der Bezüge und der Bettwäsche. Die Decke aus Kaoba im Wohnzimmer hebt sich vom Steinboden ab.

sensual elegance
sensual elegancia
une élégance sensuelle
sinnliche eleganz

PATTERNS AND TEXTURES are vital in the décor. There are many textiles that are soft to the touch, such as velvet, satin and silk. The wood's veining and the stone table in the dining room are the most appealing features in this area, while the living room, bedroom and study are dominated by the pattern of the rugs. Their stylishness is emphasized by the height of the walls and the finish of the cornices and pedestals.

EL ESTAMPADO Y LA TEXTURA tienen un papel decisivo en la decoración. Abundan textiles suaves al tacto como el terciopelo, el satín y la seda. Los veteados de la madera y la mesa pétrea del comedor se convierten en el atractivo de esta zona; mientras que en la sala, la habitación y el estudio, es el dibujo de los tapetes lo que sobresale. La altura de los muros y el terminado de cornisas y zoclos realzan la sensación de elegancia.

MOTIFS ET TEXTURES jouent ici un rôle essentiel dans la décoration. Les tissus doux au toucher, comme le velours, le satin et la soie, abondent. Les veines naturelles du bois et de la table en marbre sont décisives pour mettre en valeur la salle à manger alors que dans le salon, la chambre et le bureau, ce sont les motifs des tapis que l'on retient. Mais cette sensation d'élégance est aussi due à la hauteur des plafonds et aux finitions des moulures et des plinthes.

MUSTER UND TEXTUR spielen eine entscheidende Rolle in der Dekoration. Es gibt reichlich weiche Stoffe wie Samt, Satin und Seide. Die Maserung des Holzes und der Steintisch des Esszimmers werden zur Attraktion dieser Bereiche; während es im Wohnzimmer, im Schlafzimmer und im Studio das Muster der Teppiche ist, das auffällt. Die Höhe der Wände und die Verarbeitung der Simse und Fussleisten heben den Eindruck von Eleganz hervor.

scale and proportion
escala y proporción
à la même échelle
masstab und proportion

MAKING SURE all the different items of furniture in an apartment are in proportion and in scale is a failsafe option. Cushions, plants, adornments and other objects have been added with this balance in mind. This home offers a notable contrast with its urban and tree-filled views.

ES GENIAL que, pese a tratarse de piezas sueltas, todos los muebles que hay en el apartamento guardan proporción entre sí, descollando como un conjunto a la misma escala. Con esta misma gracia y armonía han sido ubicados cojines, plantas, adornos y otros objetos. Un hogar que ejerce un fuerte contraste ante una vista muy urbana y arbolada.

BIEN QUE COMPOSÉ de pièces d'origine variée, les décorateurs ont eu l'idée géniale de soigner les proportions du mobilier de l'appartement pour qu'il forme un tout à la même échelle. Pour couronner cette harmonie, ils ont placé ici et là des coussins, des plantes, des objets décoratifs afin de faire contraster les lieux avec la vue donnant sur un paysage arborisé et très urbain.

ES IST GENIAL, dass, obwohl es sich um Einzelstücke handelt, alle Möbel der Wohnung in Proportion zueinander stehen, als Ensemble im gleichen Masstab auftreten. Mit der gleichen Grazie und Harmonie wurden Kissen, Pflanzen, Zierobjekte und andere Stücke platziert. Ein Heim, das in starkem Gegensatz zu der sehr städtischen Aussicht steht.

marked rhythm
ritmo protagónico
un rythme prépondérant
hauptsache rhythmus

THIS PLACE HAS BEEN DECORATED using components of great visual prowess thanks to its spatial quality. Many of these components come in pairs (two seats, two armchairs, two vases, two chaise longues), giving the décor a marked rhythm. Other prominent objects include the bust, chandeliers and coffee table, while the lead role in the rest area has been taken by the bed itself.

LA DECORACIÓN DEL LUGAR posee elementos de gran peso visual; ello es posible gracias a la calidad espacial. Muchos de estos elementos son introducidos en pares (dos sillas, dos sillones, dos jarrones, dos chaise longues), lo que provoca que la decoración tenga un ritmo. Hay otros protagonistas diversificados como son el busto, los candiles y la mesa central de la sala, en cambio, el espacio de descanso tiene como pieza estelar a la propia cama.

PARCE QUE L'ESPACE EST DE QUALITÉ, il a été possible pour la décoration d'utiliser des éléments qui attirent l'œil. Beaucoup d'entre eux vont par paire (chaises, fauteuils, grands vases, canapés chaises longues), ce qui donne du rythme à la décoration. Divers autres éléments jouent également un grand rôle comme le buste sculpté, les lustres ou la table au centre du salon. En revanche, la chambre ne renferme qu'une seule pièce jouant un rôle majeur : le lit.

DIE DEKORATION dieses Ortes besitzt Elemente mit grossem optischem Gewicht; dank der räumlichen Eigenschaften ist das möglich. Viele dieser Elemente werden in Paaren präsentiert (zwei Stühle, zwei Sessel, zwei Krüge, zwei Chaise Longue), was der Dekoration Rhythmus verleiht. Es gibt verschiedene andere Hauptdarsteller wie die Büste, der Kronleuchter und der Tisch im Zentrum des Wohnzimmers, während im Ruhebereich das Bett selbst die Hauptrolle spielt.

practical and comfortable

funcional y confortable

fonctionnelle et confortable

funktional und bequem

WITHOUT BEING OVER-AMBITIOUS, the rugs make an important esthetic contribution to this apartment and reveal great decorative potential. The simplicity of their fabric and colors enables them to combine well with the different floor surfaces. The bedroom is transformed into a warm vault with the bed in the middle by the rug, wall and wooden floor. Another feature of this room is its highly polished and shiny surfaces.

SIN EL INTENTO DE PROTAGONIZAR, los tapetes le dan un sentido a la estética de este departamento y se muestran como accesorios potencialmente decorativos. La sobriedad de sus tejidos y colores facilita su combinación con los diversos recubrimientos usados en pisos. En la recámara, el tapete, el muro y el piso de madera convierten a esta pieza en una bóveda cálida con la cama al centro. Otra solución que se destaca en este interior son las superficies muy pulidas y reflejantes.

BIEN QU'ILS N'AIENT PAS LE PREMIER RÔLE, les tapis donnent un sens à l'esthétique de cet appartement en prouvant qu'ils peuvent être aussi des accessoires très décoratifs. La sobriété de leurs tissus et couleurs facilitent leur association avec les divers revêtements employés au sol. Dans la chambre, le tapis, le mur et le parquet transforment cette pièce en nid douillet avec son lit au centre. Autre solution suggérée par cet appartement : des surfaces très lisses et réfléchissant la lumière.

OHNE DEN VERSUCH SICH IN DEN VORDERGRUND ZU DRÄNGEN, verleihen die Teppiche der Ästhetik dieser Wohnung Sinn und sie präsentieren sich als mögliches dekoratives Extra. Die Nüchternheit ihres Gewebes und und ihrer Farben erleichtert die Kombination mit verschiedenen Bodenbeschichtungen. Im Schlafzimmer verwandeln der Teppich, die Wand und der Holzboden den Raum in ein warmes Gewölbe mit einem Bett im Zentrum. Eine andere Lösung, die in dieser Inneneinrichtung heraussticht, sind die stark glänzenden und reflektierenden Oberflächen.

An oval table was chosen to make the most of the dining room's rectangular layout. Its surface looks splendid and contrasts with the tone of the seats. The carving unit's surface also looks great.

Para sacar provecho de la planta rectangular del comedor se selecciona una mesa ovalada, cuya cubierta sobresale por su estética y actúa por contraste con el tono de las sillas. La cubierta del trinchador es también muy lucidora.

Pour profiter de la forme rectangulaire de la salle à manger, on y a placé une table de forme ovale avec un dessus très esthétique qui contraste avec la teinte des chaises. Le dessus des placards contre le mur est également très réussi.

Um die rechteckige Fläche des Esszimmers zu nutzen wird ein ovaler Tisch gewählt, dessen Platte durch seine Ästhetik hervorsticht und als Kontrast zum Farbton der Stühle dient. Die Oberfläche der Anrichte ist auch stark glänzend.

flying towards the horizon
volando hacia el horizonte
vers l'horizon
zum horizont fliegend

The synergy between indoors and outdoors can be potentiated with a glass partition to make the most of the view, along with a terrace that just seems to swoop down on to the lake. The effect is truly spectacular.

La sinergia entre el afuera y el adentro se consiguen a partir de un barandal de vidrio que libera las vistas y una terraza que literalmente vuela hacia el lago, creando un efecto único.

Grâce à la balustrade en verre du balcon qui offre une vue dégagée et une terrasse qui nous donne littéralement l'impression de se diriger vers l'horizon, la synergie est réussie entre l'extérieur et l'intérieur.

Die Verschmelzung zwischen Innen und Aussen wird durch ein Glasgeländer erreicht, das die Aussicht frei lässt und eine Terrasse, die wörtlich zum Horizont fliegt, somit einen einzigartigen Effekt schaffend.

Earth and wood tones proudly display their natural origins and add character to the public areas. The private areas boast a subtle chestnut ambience with blue tones standing out.

Los colores térreos y los de las maderas recuerdan su origen natural, dotando a las zonas públicas de carácter. Las áreas privadas mantienen una sutil atmósfera castaña, sobre la que destacan tonos de azul.

Les couleurs de la pierre et du bois nous rappellent leur origine naturelle et donnent du caractère aux pièces communes. Dans les pièces privées, le marron fait subtilement ressortir les reflets du bleu.

Die Erdfarben und die Farben des Holzes erinnern an seine natürliche Herkunft, den öffentlichen Bereichen Charakter gebend. Die privaten Bereiche bewahren durch die Kastanienfarbe eine subtile Atmosphäre, in der die Blautöne hervorstechen.

THE CLEAN DESIGN AND SIMPLE DÉCOR grant nature the lead role. Transparencies dominate a space that houses only the essentials. The area with the jacuzzi, basins and bathtubs has been unified in a functional continuum. Four eye-catching mirrors reflect images of the natural surroundings evolving over the course of the day.

LA LIMPIEZA DEL DISEÑO Y LA SOBRIEDAD DE LA DECORACIÓN admiten que la naturaleza tenga el rol principal. Las transparencias dominan un espacio donde sólo existe lo indispensable. La zona de jacuzzi, lavabos y tina se ha unido en un todo continuo funcional. Llaman la atención los cuatro espejos en los que se reflejan imágenes del entorno natural, que van cambiando con el transcurrir del día.

AVEC UN DESIGN NET ET UNE DÉCORATION SOBRE, la nature peut jouer le premier rôle. Ici, les transparences dominent l'espace qui ne contient uniquement que l'indispensable. Le jacuzzi, les lavabos et la baignoire sont regroupés dans la même zone continue pour faciliter leur utilisation. Les quatre miroirs qui réfléchissent le paysage environnant évoluant au fil de la journée attirent particulièrement l'œil.

DIE REINHEIT DES DESIGNS UND NÜCHTERNHEIT IN DER DEKORATION erlauben der Natur die Hauptrolle zu spielen. Transparenz herrscht in einem Raum vor, in dem sich nur das nötigste befindet. Die Zone des Jacuzzi, der Waschbecken und der Badewanne sind in einer funktionellen Konstante verbunden. Die vier Spiegel, die im Laufe des Tages sich verändernde Bilder der umgebenen Natur reflektieren, erregen Aufmerksamkeit.

natural reflection
reflejo natural
reflet naturel
natürliche reflektion

continuous isles
islas continuas
une succession de coins
fortlaufende inseln

THIS APARTMENT IS MORE FORMAL INDOORS THAN OUTSIDE but its esthetic style is unchanging. Neutral tones dominate the larger surfaces, with blue and green for the details, to evoke peace and freshness. The social area is extensively furnished, creating an unbroken archipelago of isles from the living room to the terrace. Modules affording greater flexibility are the choice for the armchairs, tables, seats and stools.

CON MAYOR FORMALIDAD AL INTERIOR QUE AL EXTERIOR, este departamento conserva una estética uniforme. El dominio de tonos neutros en las grandes superficies y azul y verde en los detalles, evoca tranquilidad y frescura. El área social ha sido súper amueblada, creando una continuidad de islas desde la sala hasta la terraza. Para sillones, mesas, sillas y bancas se opta por módulos que permiten flexibilidad en el amueblado.

PLUS FORMEL À L'INTÉRIEUR QUE DEHORS, cet appartement se caractérise par une esthétique uniforme. Les tons neutres dominent les grandes surfaces alors que le vert et le bleu des détails apportent une touche de fraîcheur et de calme. Les meubles dans la pièce commune sont très nombreux afin d'aménager plusieurs coins à part, du salon à la terrasse. Et les fauteuils, chaises, tables et tabourets sont tous modulaires pour s'adapter à toute nouvelle disposition.

MIT MEHR FORMALITÄT IM INNENBEREICH ALS IM AUSSENBEREICH bewahrt diese Wohnung eine gleichmässige Ästhetik. Die Vorherrschaft neutraler Töne auf den grossen Flächen und Blau und Grün in den Details, erweckt Ruhe und Frische. Der Gesellschaftsbereich wurde hervorragend möbliert, fortlaufende Inseln vom Wohnzimmer bis auf die Terrasse schaffend. Bei Sesseln, Tischen, Stühlen und Hockern werden Einheiten gewählt, die Flexibilität in der Möblierung ermöglichen.

illusion in light
ilusión en luz
l'illusion de la lumière
illusion in licht

THE OVERALL AMBIENCE is virtually monochrome. Items with repeated forms are used, and the lighting is a central factor. A mixture of green, yellow and white light is displayed on the living room's different planes. A selection of paintings by contemporary Mexican artists decorates the living and dining rooms, while the bedroom is characterized more by its austerity.

EL AMBIENTE GENERAL es casi monocromático. Destaca el uso de elementos en los que hay una repetición de formas. La iluminación es un factor esencial. Una mezcla de luz verde, amarilla y blanca se despliega en los planos diferentes del salón. Selectos cuadros de artistas mexicanos contemporáneos se yerguen en la sala y el comedor, mientras que la habitación conserva un aire más austero.

L'AMBIANCE GÉNÉRALE est presque monochrome et on remarquera la répétition des formes pour certains éléments. L'éclairage, un mélange de lumières verte, jaune et blanche, joue un rôle essentiel en se déployant sur divers surfaces du salon. Des tableaux bien choisis d'artistes contemporains mexicains se dressent ici et là dans le séjour et la salle à manger alors que, pour la chambre, on opte pour une atmosphère plus austère.

DAS ALLGEMEINE AMBIENTE ist fast einfarbig. Es ragt die Verwendung von Elementen, die sich in der Form wiederholen, heraus. Die Beleuchtung ist ein wesentlicher Faktor. Eine Mischung aus grünem, gelbem und weissem Licht breitet sich von den verschiedenen Ebenen des Wohnzimmers aus. Ausgesuchte Gemälde zeitgenössischer mexikanischer Künstler sind im Wohnzimmer und im Esszimmer ausgestellt, während das Schlafzimmer einen schmuckloseren Eindruck bewahrt.

A wall with a metallic finish is an original way of separating the study from the bar, and the light brings out its rugged texture. The furniture is light and discrete, except for the onyx bar which is lit from the inside.

Un muro metalizado sirve para dividir con originalidad el estudio del bar, su rugosa textura resalta con la luz. El mobiliario es ligero y discreto, con excepción de la barra de ónix que ha sido iluminada por dentro.

Un mur métallisé, avec sa texture qui fait ressortir la lumière, divise de manière originale le bureau du coin-bar. Le mobilier reste léger et discret à l'exception du comptoir en onyx qui est éclairé de l'intérieur.

Eine metallene Mauer dient als originelle Trennung zwischen dem Studio und der Bar, seine raue Textur wird durch das Licht betont. Die Möbel sind leicht und diskret, mit Ausnahme der Onyxtheke die von innen beleuchtet wird.

THE DIAGONAL ARRANGEMENT OF ALL THE FLOORS is a decorative constant in this apartment, as is the presence of circular shapes in the living room's ornaments and artwork. When the lights in the onyx bar are switched on, its peculiar and attractive veining creates a landscape awash with spheres.

LA COLOCACIÓN DE TODOS LOS PISOS EN DIAGONAL es una constante decorativa en este apartamento, así como la inclusión de formas circulares en los objetos de ornato y arte de la sala. Cuando está encendido el muro de ónix del bar, su peculiar y hermoso veteado reconstruye un paisaje plagado de esferas.

LES LIGNES DIAGONALES des revêtements pour tous les sols de l'appartement homogénéisent la décoration à laquelle s'ajoutent des objets ou des œuvres d'art de forme ronde dans le salon. Lorsqu'il est éclairé, le mur en onyx du coin-bar, avec ses veines naturelles si particulières et si belles, offre le spectacle d'un paysage couvert de sphères.

EINE KONSTANTE IN DER DEKORATION SIND DIE DIAGONAL VERLEGTEN Böden in dieser Wohnung, sowie auch die runden Formen in den Zier- und Kunstobjekten des Wohnzimmers. Wenn die Onyxwand der Bar angeschaltet ist, schafft seine einzigartige und wunderschöne Maserung eine Landschaft die von Kugeln zu strotzen scheint.

esthetic arrangement
conjunto estético
une composition esthétique
ästhetisches ensemble

THE LIVING ROOM'S SLIDING DOOR SYSTEM opens up some exceptional views. Sun beds, sofas, tabourets and armchairs are arranged in a single line, creating a very appealing overall effect. Surfaces in the bathroom are finished with stone, in contrast with the design of the washbasin and the large mirror that stretches from one wall to the other, to enhance the sensation of spaciousness. Bedroom accessories come in bright red toned with light brown.

EL SISTEMA DE PUERTAS CORREDIZAS de la estancia hace que el dominio de las vistas sea excepcional. Camastros, sofás, taburetes y sillones comparten una misma línea, lo que convierte en altamente estético el conjunto. El baño está recubierto de materiales pétreos, distinguiéndose el diseño de los lavamanos y el gran espejo que cruza de muro a muro, para aumentar la impresión de amplitud. Los accesorios de la habitación son de un rojo enérgico, que se matiza con el tabaco.

LE FAIT QUE LE SÉJOUR SOIT DOTÉ DE PORTES COULISSANTES permet de profiter de la vue exceptionnelle. Les chaises longues, canapés, tabourets et fauteuils sont tous de style identique pour donner naissance à une véritable composition esthétique. La salle de bain est tout en pierre et on remarquera le design des lavabos et le grand miroir qui va d'un mur à l'autre afin d'agrandir la pièce. Quant aux accessoires dans la chambre, ils sont d'un rouge dont la vivacité s'atténue avec le marron.

DIE VERWENDETEN SCHIEBETÜREN des Wohnzimmers lassen die Dominanz der Aussicht ausserordentlich wirken. Liegen, Sofas, Hocker und Sessel teilen die gleiche Linie, was das Ensemble extrem ästhetisch wirken lässt. Das Badezimmer ist mit Materialien aus Stein beschichtet, das Design der Waschbecken und der grosse Spiegel, der, um den Eindruck von Weite zu verstärken, von Wand zu Wand reicht, stechen hervor. Die dekorativen Elemente im Schlafzimmer sind von einem energischen Rot, das durch den Tabakton gemildert wird.

visual magic
mágicas visuales
des créations visuelles magiques
optische magie

THE VISUAL ASPECT IS SUPERB and the architectural solution is wonderful, framing the huge rock on view outside like a cinema screen. This spectacular effect can be seen from two different heights. The dining room comprises a sleek table and wire seats, and has a space for resting. The terrace furniture is delicate and light.

LA VISUAL ES ESTUPENDA y la solución arquitectónica soberbia al enmarcar como si fuera una pantalla de cine, la enorme roca que compone el paisaje marino. Este espectáculo se puede observar desde las dos alturas. El comedor se conforma por una esbelta mesa y sillas Wire, y cuenta con un espacio para reposar. El mobiliario de la terraza es delicado y liviano.

ÉTANT DONNÉ QUE LA VUE EST MAGNIFIQUE, la décoration reste sobre pour se contenter de l'entourer comme s'il s'agissait de reproduire sur un écran de cinéma l'énorme rocher qui domine ce paysage de bord de mer. On peut d'ailleurs admirer ce dernier à deux hauteurs différentes. La salle à manger comporte de fines chaises et une table Wire ainsi qu'un coin-repos. Quant au mobilier de la terrasse, il est délicat et léger.

DIE SICHT IST GROSSARTIG UND DIE ARCHITEKTONISCHE LÖSUNG hervorragend: den riesigen Stein, der die Meerlandschaft beherrscht, wie eine Kinoleinwand zu umrahmen. Dieses Ereignis kann man von beiden Etagen betrachten. Das Esszimmer besteht aus einem schlanken Tisch und Wire Stühlen und verfügt über eine Ruhezone. Die Möbel der Terrasse sind delikat und leicht.

total minimalism
minimalismo total
minimalisme total
minimalismus total

THE SPACE LOOKS FREE AND UNCLUTTERED, with only the bare essentials being accommodated there. Simple geometric shapes, natural fabrics, uncomplicated language and the color of the materials themselves are what make the place stand out. The dining room ceiling is stunning. It consists of a single piece of wood and is notable for its sheer size and beauty. It is also the same tone as the wide floorboards.

EL ESPACIO LUCE LIBRE Y EXENTO DE ELEMENTOS, solamente es ocupado por lo mínimo y lo básico. Formas geométricas simples, tejidos naturales, lenguaje sencillo y el colorido de los propios materiales se distinguen. La cubierta del comedor es apabullante, está hecha de una sola pieza de madera y destaca por su dimensión y belleza; concuerda en tonalidad con los anchos tablones del piso.

DÉNUÉ DE TOUT ÉLÉMENT QUI N'EST PAS INDISPENSABLE, une grande liberté règne sur cet appartement. Des formes géométriques simples, des étoffes naturelles, un langage décoratif élémentaire et les couleurs brutes des matériaux sont mis en valeur. Le dessus de table de la salle à manger, fait à partir d'une seule pièce de bois, est stupéfiant de beauté avec ses dimensions généreuses. Ses teintes s'associent de plus merveilleusement avec les larges lattes du parquet.

DER RAUM ERSCHEINT FREI UND BEFREIT VON OBJEKTEN, er ist nur durch ein Minimum und Elementares besetzt. Einfache geometrische Formen, natürliche Stoffe, eine schlichte Sprache und die den Materialien eigenen Farben stechen heraus. Die Platte des Esstisches ist umwerfend, sie besteht aus einem einzigen Stück Holz und beeindruckt durch ihre Grösse und Schönheit; ihr Farbton passt zu den breiten Bodendielen.

THE APARTMENT is distinguished by its exquisite surfaces and the care that went into the architectural details. All the furniture is based strictly on right angles, and in the living room it is more stylish and ergonomic. The longest wall in the bedroom is used to make a discrete closet. The décor shuns ornate items.

EL APARTAMENTO se distingue por la finura en los acabados y el cuidado en el detalle constructivo. El mobiliario en su totalidad es estrictamente de ángulos rectos. El juego de sala tiene mucho estilo y es ergonómico. En la habitación, se aprovecha la pared de mayor longitud para generar un discreto clóset. El decorado evita los objetos de ornato.

CET APPARTEMENT se distingue par la finesse de ses finitions et les détails soignés de sa construction. Les angles droits dominent rigoureusement l'ensemble du mobilier. La disposition du salon est à la fois ergonomique et très stylisée. Dans la chambre, on profite de la longueur du mur pour y placer une armoire discrète et aucun objet décoratif n'y trouve place.

DIE WOHNUNG ist bemerkenswert durch die Feinheit der Verarbeitung und der Aufmerksamkeit bei baulichen Details. Die Möblierung im Ganzen besteht strikt aus rechten Winkeln. Die Sitzgruppe im Wohnzimmer hat viel Stil und ist ergonomisch. Im Schlafzimmer wird die längste Wand genutzt um einen diskreten Wandschrank zu schaffen. In der Dekoration werden Zierobjekte vermieden.

circular corners

rincones circulares

des recoins circulaires

runde ecken

THE FURNITURE ARRANGEMENT in the living / dining room is dynamic. Round and oval tables surrounded by seating are the norm. The tables' shape creates decorative circular and semicircular corners all over the living room and the terrace, all with views of the sea, turning the ocean into a part of the décor. The bedroom offers a more serene picture distinguished by the structure framing it, and the inclusion of a canopy is an option.

EN LA SALA-COMEDOR la disposición de los muebles es dinámica. Imperan las mesas redondas y ovaladas rodeadas de plazas para sentarse. La forma de las mesas genera rincones decorativos circulares y semicirculares a lo largo y ancho de la estancia y la terraza, todos con vistas hacia el mar, convirtiendo al océano en parte de la decoración. La habitación mantiene una imagen más serena, se distingue por una estructura que la enmarca y que puede o no usarse con dosel.

DANS LE SALON-SALLE à manger, la disposition des meubles se distingue par son dynamisme. Les tables rondes et ovales, entourées de sièges, dominent. La forme des tables suscite l'aménagement de différents coins décoratifs (semi-)circulaires sur toute la longueur et largeur du séjour et de la terrasse. On profite donc de la vue sur la mer et cette dernière fait partie intégrale de la décoration. La chambre conserve une apparence plus sereine et on y remarquera le baldaquin du lit qui peut être utilisé avec ou sans drapé.

IM WOHN- ESSZIMMER ist die Anordnung der Möbel dynamisch. Es herrschen runde und ovale Tische vor, die von Sitzgelegenheiten umgeben sind. Die Form der Tische schafft dekorative kreisförmige und halbkreisförmige Winkel über die Länge und über die Breite des Wohnbereiches und der Terrasse, alle mit Blick aufs Meer, den Ozean in einen Teil der Dekoration verwandelnd. Das Schlafzimmer wahrt einen beschaulicheren Eindruck, es sticht eine Rahmenstruktur hervor, die mit oder ohne Baldachin benutzt werden kann.

A LARGE RECTANGULAR JACUZZI IN THE TERRACE overlooks the beach. The view is interrupted only by a protective transparent partition and takes in the jungle and the extensive and spectacular horizon. Surfaces in this area are made with non-slip stone.

EN LA TERRAZA, UN JACUZZI RECTANGULAR de buen tamaño mira hacia la playa. La vista es interrumpida sólo por un barandal transparente que sirve para brindar protección. Desde allí se descubre el paisaje selvático y se contempla el horizonte extenso y profundo. Los acabados de esta área son pétreos y antiderrapantes.

SUR LA TERRASSE, UN JACUZZI RECTANGULAIRE de bonne taille fait face à la plage, la balustrade transparente de sécurité étant le seul élément qui interrompt légèrement la continuité visuelle. Depuis la terrasse, on peut tout de même découvrir le paysage sauvage large et profond à l'horizon. Ajoutons que cet espace est revêtu de pierre mais aussi d'éléments antidérapants.

AUF DER TERRASSE BLICKT EIN RECHTECKIGER JACUZZI guter Grösse aufs Meer. Die Sicht wird nur durch ein transparentes Geländer unterbrochen, das Sicherheit gibt. Von dort kann man die tropische Waldlandschaft entdecken und den weiten und tiefen Horizont betrachten. Die Materialien in dieser Zone sind aus Stein und rutschfestem Stein.

THE APARTMENT is crossed lengthwise by a very open wooden lattice structure that gives rise to a corridor. This same component appears again to separate the dining room from the living room, acting like a kind of shop window. The prevalence of wood over other building materials is indicative of a desire to emulate the lush landscape outside.

EL APARTAMENTO es cruzado longitudinalmente por una celosía muy abierta de madera, que da lugar a un corredor. Este mismo componente se repite para dividir la sala del comedor, haciendo también las veces de escaparate. La hegemonía de la madera sobre otros materiales constructivos revela la intención de mimetizarse con el abundante paisaje exterior.

CET APPARTEMENT est traversé dans sa longueur par une jalousie très ouverte en bois qui donne sur un couloir. On utilise de nouveau cet élément pour séparer le salon de la salle à manger où il sert, cette fois, également d'étagères vitrées. La domination du bois par rapport aux autres matériaux de construction montre que l'on a d'abord voulu s'intégrer au paysage extérieur.

DIE WOHNUNG wird längs von einer sehr offenen Holzstruktur durchquert, die einen Durchgang abteilt. Die gleiche Struktur wird wiederholt, um das Wohnzimmer vom Esszimmer zu trennen, gleichzeitig als Regal dienend. Die Dominanz des Holzes über andere Baumaterialien enthüllt den Versuch mit der reichhaltigen Landschaft zu verschmelzen.

spatial segmentation
segmentación espacial
division spatiale
räumliche unterteilung

simplicity and contrast
simplicidad y contraste
simplicité et constraste
einfachheit und kontrast

DAYLIGHT PLAYS A FUNDAMENTAL ROLE in the décor of this apartment. In the bedroom, the bed is flush with the floor, like a futon, and a decorative light emerges from the bureaus. The kitchen is blessed with fine dark lining on its shelves, which stands in contrast with the white marble surfaces. The living room is simple, orderly and defined by light tones and pure lines. Two hanging globe lamps and wallpaper with a pale pink floral pattern are its main features.

LA ILUMINACIÓN NATURAL es medular en la decoración de este departamento. En la habitación, la cama está casi a ras del suelo, como futón, y de los burós desciende una luz decorativa. La cocina se caracteriza por el fino revestimiento oscuro de sus anaqueles, contrastante con las cubiertas de mármol blanco. La sala se distingue por su simplicidad, orden, matices claros y líneas puras. Dos lámparas de bola colgantes y un murete con dibujos florales en rosa tenue conquistan la escena.

LA LUMIÈRE NATURELLE est primordiale dans la décoration de cet appartement. Dans la chambre, le lit est quasiment à ras du sol, comme un futon, et un éclairage décoratif descendant est diffusé par les tables de nuit. La cuisine se caractérise par le fin revêtement foncé de ses placards qui contraste avec le blanc du marbre. Le salon se distingue par sa simplicité, l'ordre qui y règne, les teintes claires et les lignes pures. Deux lampes suspendues en forme de boule et un pan de mur à motif floral rose pâle y jouent le premier rôle.

NATÜRLICHES LICHT ist der entscheidende Faktor in der Dekoration dieser Wohnung. Im Schlafzimmer ist das Bett fast auf Fussbodenhöhe, wie ein Futon, und von den Nachttischen fällt ein dekoratives Licht herab. Die Küche wird durch die feine dunkle Beschichtung der Schränke charakterisiert, die im Kontrast zu dem weissen Marmor der Arbeitsflächen steht. Das Wohnzimmer: der Bereich sticht durch seine Schlichtheit, seine Ordnung, helle Farbschattierungen und reine Linien hervor. Zwei runde Hängelampen und die Wandverkleidung mit Blumenmuster in zartem rosa erobern die Szenerie.

PAIRS OF OBJECTS in the living room and dining room define the cadence and symmetry of these places: two tables, two armchairs, two vases, sets of lights arranged two by two and even a double table in the middle. The bedroom follows the same scheme: two bureaus, two lamps, two sets of cushions, and even two mattresses comprising the bed. The coloring is neutral, the dominant tones being progressions towards off-white.

DUPLAS DE OBJETOS que habitan la sala y el comedor le confieren una cadencia y simetría a estos lugares: dos mesillas, dos sillones, dos jarrones, juegos de lámparas de dos en dos, y hasta doble mesa de centro. En la habitación se continúa con esta misma consonancia: dos burós, dos lámparas, dos juegos de cojines, y hasta dos colchones que conforman la cama. La cromatía es neutra, con predominio de las progresiones hacia el crema.

LES OBJETS DANS le salon et la salle à manger qui apportent rythme et symétrie aux lieux vont toujours ici par deux : chaises, fauteuils, grands vases, lampes, avec même une double table centrale. Dans la chambre, ce motif est répété : deux tables de nuit, deux lampes, deux ensembles de coussins et deux matelas pour le lit ! La gamme chromatique est neutre avec une domination des différentes nuances de crème.

OBJEKTE IN DOPPELTER Ausführung, die das Wohnzimmer und das Esszimmer beleben, geben diesen Bereichen Rhythmus und Symmetrie: zwei kleine Tische, zwei Sessel, zwei Krüge, Lampensets in zwei und zwei und sogar ein doppelter Couchtisch. Im Schlafzimmer wird weiter diesem Einklang gefolgt: zwei Nachttische, zwei Lampen, zwei Sets Kissen und sogar zwei Matratzen die das Bett bilden. Die Farbgebung ist neutral, mit Vorherrschaft der Cremefarben.

flowing symmetry
simetría cadenciosa
une symétrie rythmée
rhythmische symmetrie

peaceful and charming
apacible y con encanto
calme et charmant
friedlich und charmant

THE USE OF THE SAME WOOD all over the floor, a concise range of tones and just one type of lights in the soffit afford this apartment great uniformity. The décor is peaceful and transmits serenity. The quest for spaciousness is unrelenting. The upper areas look purged, and emptiness is part and parcel of the design's objective.

EL USO DE LA MISMA MADERA en todo el piso, de una gama reducida de matices y de un solo tipo de luminarias a plafón, le confieren uniformidad al departamento. El decorado es apacible y transmite quietud. La apuesta por la espacialidad es constante; las alturas lucen despejadas y el vacío es parte de la intención del diseño.

LE FAIT D'UTILISER LE MÊME bois pour tous les sols, une gamme réduite de couleurs et un seul type de luminaires au plafond uniformise cet appartement. La décoration transforme alors les lieux en endroit calme et tranquille. Étant donné que les espaces vides font partie du design, on privilégie ici constamment les étendues dégagées avec le haut des pièces qui reste intact.

DIE VERWENDUNG DES GLEICHEN Holzes mit beschränkten Farbschattierung für alle Böden und nur einer Form der Beleuchtung mit Deckenplatten geben der Wohnung Einheitlichkeit. Die Dekoration ist friedlich und vermittelt Ruhe. Es wird konstant auf die räumliche Grösse gesetzt; die Höhe wirkt frei und Leere ist Teil des Ziels im Design.

The backrests of the seats and armchairs are made of leather.
Two sofas in waxen tones, together with the rear wall of the
fireplace, create a dark frame that highlights an old rug that
stands out for its coloring.

La piel se introduce tanto en los respaldos de las sillas como en
los sillones. Dos sofás en tono acerado, en coordinación con el muro
de fondo de la chimenea, completan un marco oscuro para resaltar
la vista de un tapete antiguo que descuella por su color.

Le cuir recouvre ici aussi bien les dossiers de chaises que les fauteuils.
Le gris très foncé des deux canapés, qui se marie avec celui du mur
du fond où se trouve la cheminée, encadre le vieux tapis de collection
pour en faire ressortir sa couleur.

Leder wird sowohl bei den Rückenlehnen der Stühle als auch bei
den Sesseln verwendet. Zwei Sofas in Stahlgrau, zusammen mit
der Wand hinter dem Kamin, vervollständigen einen dunklen Rahmen
um den Blick auf einen antiken Teppich zu lenken, der durch seine
Farbe auffällt.

The design of the bathroom furniture is contemporary. The geometric volumes of the bathtub and the washbasin overflow with visual appeal, as is the case of the sleek faucets and drawers without handles.

Los muebles de baño son de diseño contemporáneo. Los volúmenes geométricos de la tina y los lavamanos resultan estéticos en extremo, lo mismo sucede con la esbelta grifería y los cajones ausentes de jaladeras.

Le design des meubles de la salle de bain est d'époque contemporaine. Les volumes géométriques de la baignoire et des lavabos sont d'un esthétisme renversant et c'est également le cas de la discrète robinetterie et des tiroirs dénués de poignées.

Die Badezimmermöbel sind zeitgenössisches Design. Die geometrischen Formen der Waschbecken und der Badewanne erweisen sich als extrem ästhetisch, das gleiche geschieht mit den schlanken Armaturen und den grifflosen Schubladen.

simple design
diseño depurado
un design épuré
reines design

FREEING THE SPACE OF ORNAMENTS to make the most of the double view of the sea is a wise move, especially as the apartment occupies a corner of the building. Furniture based on pure, simple lines are scattered around the living room but without obstructing the view. A sensation of cleanliness is conveyed by a highly polished white floor. The kitchen has been designed to make full use of its length, and the area is granted autonomy from the rest of the home by means of an architectural volume containing the refrigerator and storage space.

ES UN GRAN ACIERTO LIBERAR DECORATIVAMENTE el espacio para que se disfrute la doble vista hacia el mar, pues el departamento hace esquina. Muebles de líneas puras y simples se esparcen por la estancia sin interrumpir las visuales. La sensación de pulcritud se evidencia con el piso blanco de acabado muy pulido. El diseño de la cocina explota la longitud, y a través de un volumen arquitectónico que contiene el refrigerador y espacio de guardado, se aísla e independiza al área.

LIBÉRER L'ESPACE DE TOUTE DÉCORATION pour profiter de l'ample vue sur la mer constitue ici une belle réussite car cet appartement se trouve au coin d'un bâtiment. Des meubles à lignes pures et simples sont disposés ici et là mais sans gêner le regard vers l'extérieur. La sensation de pureté que l'on ressent est sans nul doute produite par le blanc du sol avec sa surface très lisse. Le design de la cuisine profite de sa grande longueur et le réfrigérateur et les placards de rangement en font une pièce indépendante.

ES IST KLUG DEN RAUM DEKORATIV ZU BEFREIEN, um sich an der doppelten Sicht aufs Meer zu erfreuen, da die Wohnung ein Eckfenster hat. Möbel mit reinen und einfachen Linien verteilen sich über den Wohnbereich, ohne die Sicht zu unterbrechen. Der Eindruck von Reinheit wird durch den weissen Boden und den glänzenden Oberflächen vermittelt. Das Design der Küche nutzt ihre Länge und ein bauliches Element, das den Kühlschrank und Stauraum enthält, trennt den Bereich ab und macht ihn unabhängig.

TRADITIONAL LIVING ROOM furniture is supplanted by oyster and white tabourets that contrast with the black carpet. The tabourets have been designed and arranged in such a way as to bestow an orderly and graceful appearance to the place, handing the lead role over to the artwork.

LA SALA TRADICIONAL es sustituida por un grupo de taburetes en tonos ostión y blanco, que resaltan contra la alfombra negra. El acomodo y el diseño de los taburetes permiten que el sitio luzca ordenado y con gracia, dejando el papel protagónico a las obras de arte.

AU SALON TRADITIONNEL, on préfèrera ici un ensemble de poufs de teintes blanche ou marron clair qui ressortent bien sur la moquette noire. La forme et la disposition de ces poufs dotent la pièce d'une certaine élégance et d'un certain ordre sans écraser par leur présence les œuvres d'art placées autour.

DIE TRADITIONELLE WOHNZIMMERGARNITUR wird durch eine Gruppe Hocker in Austern- und Weisstönen ersetzt, die sich von dem schwarzen Teppich abheben. Die Anordnung und das Design der Hocker erlauben dem Bereich ordentlich und graziös zu wirken, den Kunstwerken die Hauptrolle überlassend.

appearance and practicality

estética y funcionalidad

esthétique et fonctionnalité

ästhetik und funktion

IN ADDITION TO THEIR ORIGINAL ROLES, the fireplace, the kitchen bar and the cellar are used to section each area off from the others. This discrete segregation affords privacy for each space, but without sacrificing the idea of continuity. Spatial boundaries are also marked by different floor coverings, the design of which is exalted by the quality of the tiles, as well as their size and the aplomb with which they were laid down.

ADEMÁS DE SU FUNCIÓN ORIGINAL, la chimenea, la barra de cocina y la cava son aprovechadas para seccionar una zona de otra. Esta discreta vestibulación le otorga cierta privacidad a los espacios, sin que se pierda la idea de continuidad. Marcan también los límites inter-espaciales las diversas cubiertas de los pisos, destacando en el diseño la calidad de las losetas, su dimensión y el buen trabajo de colocación.

SANS PARLER DE LEUR FONCTIONNALITÉ, on peut utiliser une cheminée, un comptoir de cuisine et une cave à vin pour diviser l'espace. C'est un moyen de créer des endroits privés tout en maintenant une certaine continuité dans l'appartement. Des revêtements différents au sol, avec des dalles de qualité bien posées et de dimensions généreuses, peuvent également jouer le même rôle.

ZUSÄTZLICH ZU SEINER URSPRÜNGLICHEN FUNKTION, werden der Kamin, die Küchentheke und die Bar genutzt, um die einzelnen Zonen voneinander zu trennen. Diese diskrete Abteilung gewährt den Bereichen eine gewisse Privatheit ohne die Idee des Fortlaufenden zu verlieren. Die Grenzen zwischen den Bereichen werden auch von den verschiedenen Bodenbelägen markiert, die durch die Qualität der Fliesen, ihre Grösse und ihre gute Verlegung auffallen.

spaciousness and simplicity
amplitud y sobriedad
ampleur et sobriété
weite und nüchternheit

The apartment's ample spaciousness is further enhanced
by the unassuming décor. This effect is also generated thanks to
the widespread use of white-dyed wood and white-painted walls.
The furniture, including that of the bathroom, is based on exquisite lines.

La espacialidad del departamento es notable y acrecentada por la
sobriedad de la decoración. Cooperan a este mismo efecto de
amplitud el dominio de la madera entintada en blanco y los muros
también pintados en blanco. El diseño del mobiliario, incluso el
del baño, es de líneas exquisitas.

Les vastes dimensions de cet appartement attirent immédiatement
notre attention et la simplicité de la décoration ne fait que les mettre
en valeur. La domination du bois peint en blanc et des murs de
même couleur renforce encore cette sensation. Le design du mobilier,
avec ses lignes particulières, y compris pour la salle de bain,
constitue une réussite totale.

Die räumliche Grösse der Wohnung ist bemerkenswert und wird
durch die nüchterne Dekoration noch verstärkt. Zu diesem Effekt von
Weite tragen die Vorherrschaft weiss gefärbten Holzes und die weiss
gestrichenen Wände bei. Das Design der Möbel, einschliesslich der
des Badezimmers, ist von erlesenen Formen geprägt.

architecture arquitectónicos architectoniques architekten

10 (left) *architectural project:* ARCHETONIC, jacobo micha mizrahi, *contributors:* ernesto rossell zanotelli, alejandro rabiela salinas, alfredo muñoz jiménez y dulce karina zúñiga

11 (right) *architectural project:* ARQUITECTURA EN MOVIMIENTO

16-23 *architectural project:* ARQUITECTURA EN MOVIMIENTO

46-49 *architectural and interior design project:* BOSCO ARQUITECTOS, bosco gutiérrez cortina

70-75 *architectural project:* ARQUITECTURA PICCIOTO ARQUITECTOS, *interior design project:* LAZZA DESIGN STUDIO ARQUITECTURA, jaime lavin zavala

80-85 *architectural and interior design project:* CIBRIAN ARQUITECTOS, fernando cibrian castro

100-105 *architectural project:* ARKETIPO, flavio velázquez

106-109 *architectural project:* SERRANO Y MONJARAZ ARQUITECTOS Y T.A.C. ARQUITECTOS, *interior design project:* IDEA NARANJA / INVITO MUEBLES, anna grendys / sergio rincón, *contributors:* pia cozzi y verónica rincón

138-143 *architectural project:* PAOLA CALZADA ARQUITECTOS, paola calzada

144-149 *interior design project:* DECORÉ INTERIORISMO / TORBELI, maría patricia díaz de león / elena talavera autrique, *architectural project:* javier sordo madaleno, *contributors:* mario hallat díaz de león y mauricio hallat díaz de león

150-155 *architectural and interior design project:* GRUPO 7 ARQUITECTURA Y DISEÑO, mauricio guitiérrez losada y jorge o. vázquez rendón

156-157 *architectural project:* ARCHETONIC, jacobo micha mizrahi, *contributors:* ernesto rossell zanotelli, alejandro rabiela salinas, alfredo muñoz jiménez y dulce karina zúñiga

158-165 *interior design project:* TEXTURA®, walter allen, *architectural project:* jacobo gudiño, *contributors:* paolo rindone

166-171 *architectural project:* ZD+A DESARROLLO + ARQUITETURA, yuri zagorin alazraki y felipe buendía hegewisch, *contributors:* jorge lópez gordillo y verónica gonzález, *construction:* fernando reynoso monroy, francisco vargas y luís romero blancas

172-177 *interior design project:* TORBELI, elena talavera autrique, *architectural project:* ROJAS ARQUITECTOS, ricardo rojas, *contributors:* alberto burello, martha lópez y carmen escutia

182-187 *interior design project:* TORBELI, elena talavera autrique, *architectural project:* PARQUE REFORMA, *contributors:* carmen escutia solis y martha a. lópez reséndiz

188-193 *architectural and interior design project:* enrique martorell gutiérrez, *contributors:* alejandro de noriega d´hyver de las deses y manuel cervantes

194-201 *interior design project:* DECORÉ INTERIORISMO, mario hallat díaz de león y mauricio hallat díaz de león, *contributors:* maría patricia díaz de león girón, maría elena girón aragón, diana bautista cabello y nancy lópez terán

202-205 *architectural project:* JSª, javier sánchez corral, irvine torres, juan reyes, héctor hernández y francisco de la concha, *engineering:* JPR + JSª, fernando valdivia y sergio barrios

212-219 *architectural and interior design project:* ESPIÑEIRA I MURO Y ASOCIADOS

220-223 *architectural and interior design project:* GRUPO 7 ARQUITECTURA Y DISEÑO, mauricio guitiérrez losada y jorge o. vázquez rendón

224-227 *interior design project:* OLIMPIC KITCHEN AND FURNITURE COLLECTION

photography fotográficos photographiques fotografen

adriana cabrera ochoa - pgs. 150-155, 220-223

alberto moreno - pgs. 48-49

aldo moreno - pg. 156

© beta-plus publishing - pgs. 3-5, 8-9, 10 (right), 11 (left),

14-15, 24-45, 50-69, 76-79, 86-99, 111-137, 180-181, 206-211,

228-257, 260-261

bosco guitiérrez cortina - pgs. 48-49

carlos medina vega - pgs. 101-105

carlos soto - pgs. 158-165

cecilia del olmo - pgs. 144-149,172-177, 194-201

david chavolla - pgs. 71-75

eduardo hirose - pgs. 202-205

ernesto muñiz - pgs. 212-219

héctor flora - pgs. 158-165

jaime navarro - pgs. 138-143, 166-171

jorge silva - pgs. 188-193

josé gonzález - pgs. 80-85

juan josé díaz infante - pgs. 182-187

martha lilián tinoco - pgs. 144-149, 172-177, 194-201

nancy ambe - pgs. 158-165

olimpic kitchen and furniture collection - pgs. 225-227

rafael gamo - pgs. 10 (left), 11 (right), 16-23

virro borja - pgs. 106-109

Editado en Junio 2010. Impreso en China. El cuidado de
esta edición estuvo a cargo de AM Editores, S.A. de C.V.
Edited in June 2010. Printed in China. Published by
AM Editores, S.A. de C.V.